I0797648

BERHERT
5,97e+24
5,97e+24
5,97e+24
5,97e+24
5,97e+24
5,97e+24
5,97e+24
Berhert
MILANO
46
046
CLICKS TO JUMP POINT.
SYT-79V
T SYSTEMS ONLINE
SUPPORT ENABLED
MED-2.1
71
MED-2.1.2
72
MED-2.1.3
73

MARVEL STUDIOS
THE INFINITY SAGA
THE ART OF
MARVEL STUDIOS
GUARDIANS OF THE GALAXY VOL. 2
WRITTEN BY
JACOB JOHNSTON
FOREWORD BY
JAMES GUNN
AFTERWORD AND DUSTJACKET ART BY
ANDY PARK
BOOK DESIGN BY
ADAM DEL RE
PROJECT MANAGER
ALEX SCHARF
TITAN BOOKS

FOR MARVEL PUBLISHING
JEFF YOUNGQUIST, Editor
SARAH SINGER, Editor, Special Projects
JEREMY WEST, Manager, Licensed Publishing
SVEN LARSEN, VP, Licensed Publishing
DAVID GABRIEL, VP, Print & Digital Publishing
C.B. CEBULSKI, Editor in Chief

FOR MARVEL STUDIOS 2017
KEVIN FEIGE, President
LOUIS D'ESPOSITO, Co-President
VICTORIA ALONSO, Executive Vice President, Visual Effects
JONATHAN SCHWARTZ, Vice President, Production & Development
WILL CORONA PILGRIM, Creative Director, Research & Development
RYAN POTTER, VP Business Affairs
ERIKA DENTON, Clearances Director
RANDY McGOWAN, VP Technical Operations
AXEL SCHARF, Production Asset Manager
DAVID GRANT, Vice President, Physical Production
ALEXIS AUDITORE, Manager, Physical Assets

MARVEL STUDIOS' THE INFINITY SAGA - GUARDIANS OF THE GALAXY VOL. 2: THE ART OF THE MOVIE

ISBN: 9781803368467

First edition: July 2025

10 9 8 7 6 5 4 3 2 1

Published by Titan Books
A division of Titan Publishing Group Ltd
144 Southwark St, London SE1 0UP

www.titanbooks.com

EU RP (for authorities only)
eucomply OÜ Pärnu mnt 139b-14 11317
Talinn, Estonia
hello@eucompliancepartner.com
+3375690241

Did you enjoy this book? We love to hear from our readers. Please e-mail us at: readerfeedback@titanemail.com or write to Reader Feedback at the above address.

To receive advance information, news, competitions, and exclusive offers online, please sign up for the Titan newsletter on our website: www.titanbooks.com

A CIP catalogue record for this title is available from the British Library.

Printed in India

previous DICKINSON

FUENTEBELLA

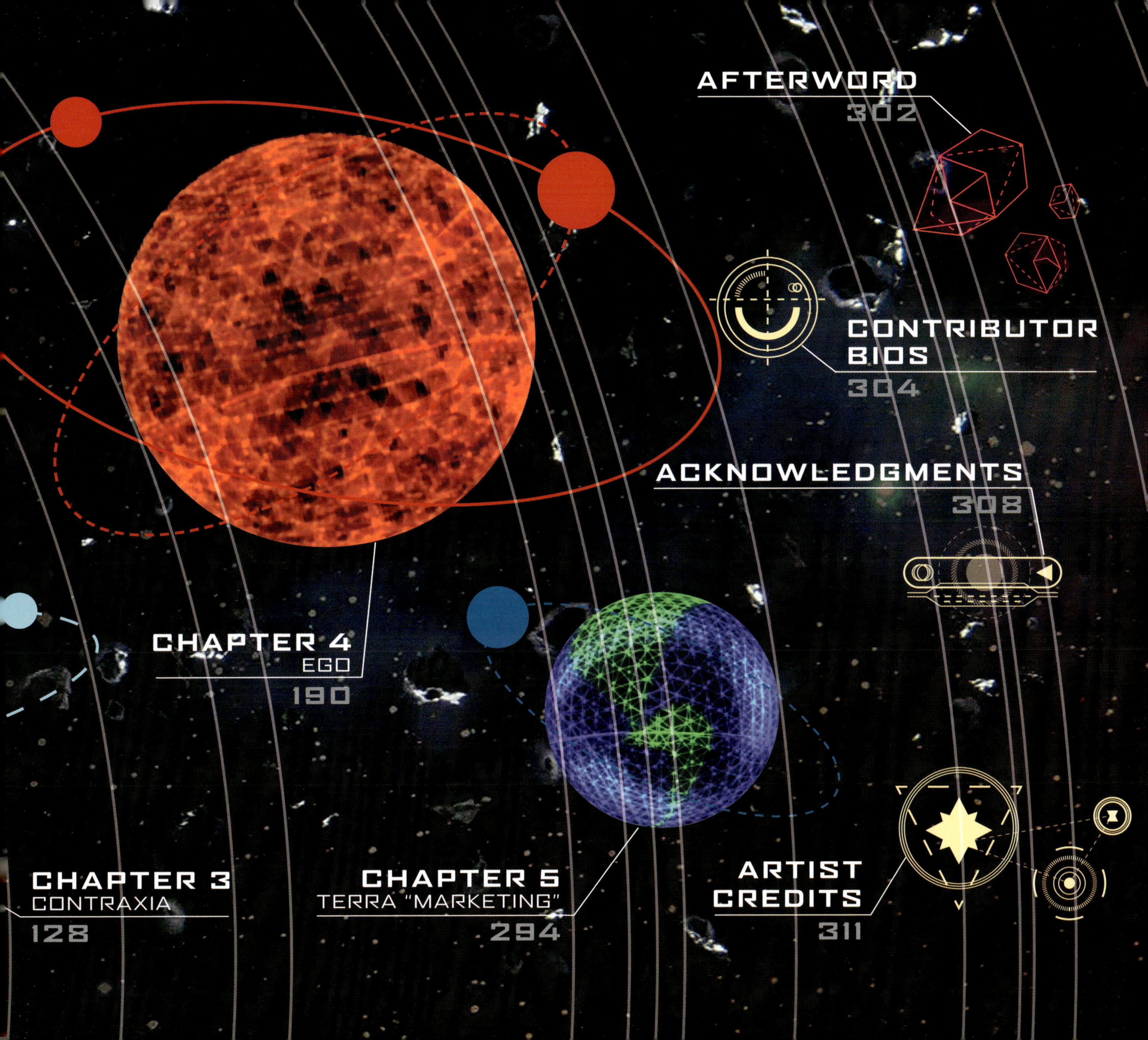

FOREWORD 2017

IN MAKING *Guardians of the Galaxy Vol. 2*, we could have done the easy thing—that thing that so many sequels do—and just remade the first film with slightly different plot points. But the only tradition of the Guardians is that we give people the thing they don't expect. So for *Vol. 2*, we created a film that was richer and deeper, and was centered around the Guardians as a group more so than just Star-Lord. But where I think we took the greatest risk was visually. I wanted people to be able to watch any scene from *Vol. 2* and know that it was a different movie with a different look and feel than *Vol. 1*. I wanted it to be more explosively colorful, more outlandishly science fiction, and more rooted in pulp art and the space-opera films of the fifties and sixties. I put together a lookbook of visual cues containing old *Amazing Stories* covers; Al Williamson and Jim Starlin art; photographs I took in Havana of the colorful, weathered buildings there; frames from 1980s *Flash Gordon* and Wong Kar-wai films; and so much more.

Luckily, I had a wonderful team of professionals around me to help fulfill this vision, to take the Guardians boldly where no raccoon has gone before.

First and foremost is Christopher Townsend, our visual effects supervisor, and the entire visual effects teams from Framestore, Weta, Trixter, Method, Animal Logic, Scanline, Lola, Luma, and Cantina Creative, and our in-house folks. More than any other Marvel movies, these people had the most profound impact on overall look, character design, set design, and cinematography. A movie of this size—taking place largely within a living planet—is simply not possible with practical sets, but must be built with computer graphics. The interior of Ego is probably the largest VFX set of all time, composed of over a trillion polygons. These people tackled this Herculean task with creativity and courageousness.

Andy Park was the head of our Visual Development team on *Vol. 2*. He and his team were responsible for many of the characters in the film—and it's the characters that are responsible for any success the Guardians have.

Scott Chambliss was our production designer who built enormous, beautiful sets in support of the vision. The interior of the Ravagers' ship, the Eclector, was composed of many attached rooms at a convention center because it was too big for any soundstages. It would take minutes to walk from one end to the other.

Hal Tenny's 3D fractal Mandelbrot set artwork was such a huge influence on our conception of Ego's planet that we hired him to help design the world.

Judianna Makovsky was our costume designer. Her exquisite eye for detail and ability to make gravity-defying costumes is without parallel. Of special note is how hard she worked to create Ayesha's costume in her lair, the most beautiful costume I've ever seen up close, and how she worked with Scott to make it connected to her throne.

Henry Braham was our cinematographer who brought so many of these looks together with his use of light and deftness of movement.

Our prosthetic team at Legacy Effects—led by Brian Sipe—not only created new aliens and characters that inhabited our galaxy, but also brought new technologies to previous characters like Drax and Gamora that made them look better and easier to manage. (On the first movie, it took Dave Bautista nearly five hours every day to have the Drax makeup applied; on the second film, it took under two hours.)

Our storyboard artists—Bryan Andrews, Darrin Denlinger, and David Krentz—are troopers of the highest order who took my rectangles with sub-stick-figures and transformed them into little pieces of art that guided our entire expedition.

And finally, I cannot express my gratitude enough for my Marvel partners—Kevin Feige, Lou D'Esposito, Victoria Alonso, and Jonathan Schwartz—and my associate producer, Simon Hatt. Like the Guardians, we were thrust together over *Vol. 1*, but truly became a family on *Vol. 2*.

This book is the story of the journey to the finished look of *Guardians of the Galaxy Vol. 2*. I hope you enjoy reading it as much as I enjoyed taking it.

We are Groot.

James Gunn
3.12.17

WELCOME BACK, A-HOLES...

DEFYING EXPECTATIONS, a band of misfits won over audiences everywhere and proudly joined their super-hero brethren in the ever-expanding Marvel Cinematic Universe. The members of this ragtag team—a Terran con man, a relentless assassin, a pumped-up brawler, a cantankerous talking raccoon, and an overly empathetic tree—were the center of an epic space opera instead of its sidebar. It was a risk everyone at Marvel Studios is sure to acknowledge—but one that paid off in more than box-office returns.

The sequels for most hit films don't come easy—but according to Writer/Director James Gunn, cracking the code for *Guardians* was simpler the second time around. Gunn's confidence came from equal parts experience and time. "People keep asking me, 'Don't you feel a lot more pressure now that the first one was so well received, that it was such a big hit?' And I'm like, 'Are you kidding me?!' I woke up at three o'clock in the morning all the time with the first movie, worried that I was making the weirdest, strangest movie that no one was going to get and it would bomb," Gunn says. "I didn't have that fear this time around. I know people are ready for this movie. I know people want to see it. People have already fallen in love with the characters.

"I know which actors are playing the characters this time," he says. "I know how to write for them better. So for me, it's been absolute pure joy this time around. The entire creation process—working with [Marvel Studios President] Kevin [Feige], with Marvel—has been great. I think if anything I had this strange anxiety of something going wrong because things really flowed and went very smoothly. I also had a lot more time to write the screenplay this time around. I had already taken a lot of notes, but I'd actually started writing the treatment the day the first movie came out. That was a huge benefit."

"You follow the characters," Executive Producer Jonathan Schwartz says. "I think the characters tell you where they want to go because all these characters have their own journeys to go down and their own damage to work through. The end point for any new story is what's the next chapter in these characters' lives."

In Marvel's *Guardians of the Galaxy*, our heroes banded together to stop Ronan and save the galaxy from an object of limitless power. What story could possibly measure up, in terms of stakes, to facing off against an enemy wielding one of the most formidable Infinity Stones? "We're definitely picking up some threads that were laid at the end of the first movie and following those story threads into the sequel," Executive Producer Louis D'Esposito says. "Of course there are new elements, characters, and challenges that they'll face—but it's all about the journey. It's always about the journey."

One of those story threads involves Peter Quill's father. "*Guardians of the Galaxy*, thematically, was very much about finding this ragtag adopted family that became the Guardians who were all kind of the last of their kind and alone in the universe," Schwartz says. "When Quill finds out that he does have a biological father out there, what does that mean for this adopted surrogate family? What does it mean to have Quill follow that story and find that character? The really fun thing about that character is it's not who you expect. He doesn't turn up the way you expect. It's a really interesting, classic character from the Guardians' cosmic mythology, but probably not the one you're thinking of."

In the comics, Peter Quill's father is J'Son, emperor of the planet Spartax. In

EGO THE LIVING PLANET

JOHN BYRNE and BOB SHAREN

J'SON OF SPARTAX

STEVE MCNIVEN, JOHN DELL, and JUSTIN PONSOR

Guardians of the Galaxy Vol. 2, Star-Lord's father is based on an altogether different comic-book character: Ego the Living Planet. Veteran actor Kurt Russell plays Ego, a character who easily beguiles his son, preying on Quill's flawed perspective. "Yondu became his surrogate father early on, a strange creature who in many ways is horrible to him," Russell says. "It only adds to Quill's ability to build up and put on a pedestal someone who he doesn't know. When Quill finally gets to meet his father, he's thrilled, he's fascinated—he is enamored with the prowess and power, and ultimately that leads Quill to a place he can be easily manipulated."

"He seems like the perfect guy," Gunn says. "He's the David Hasselhoff that Peter Quill longed to have as a father his entire life. This is the primary story, learning that the thing that we think we want—that we're going to get outside of ourselves and outside of the relationships we have—has been there all along. It's a great deal about fatherhood. With Gamora and Nebula, their father, Thanos, is the one that pitted them against each other, which caused all those problems. We have a relationship between Rocket and Yondu where Yondu starts to become a father figure to Rocket. Here's a little guy who has only been raised by scientists—he's never known any type of father—and he gets to know Yondu, whom he's so similar to in so many ways. They're both completely misused and abused their entire lives. Then there's Baby Groot and his relationship to Quill and Drax, and how they're substitute fathers for him, and what their relationship is like to that child. The movie isn't just about a villain who is trying to take over the universe—which he is trying to do—but rather it's about Quill's relationship to his dad and why his dad is doing that, what his situation is."

Adding to the colorful cast of characters is Ego's right hand, the empathic Mantis. "She's a classic character who has popped up a lot for years and years in the comics, and very recently she was a part of the Guardians of the Galaxy," Schwartz says. "In the comics, she's a Celestial Madonna, an empathic alien—and we really wanted to explore that in the film. Mantis forms a unique bond with Drax because he has lost his family, he has all this sadness within him, and with Mantis' powers she's able to really relate to him and understand his sadness. It evolves into this father/daughter relationship that's really compelling in a lot of ways. She's also a great catalyst, as she can sense what you're thinking, what's on your mind—and all of the Guardians have secrets they'd rather not air. There's a lot of dirty laundry. Mantis definitely isn't shy about airing it all out; it creates conflict with our characters, but at the end of the day also brings them closer together."

Another important step in crafting a well-balanced sequel involved peeling back the Guardians' sarcasm, grief, and preconceived notions; developing their relationships; and heightening their personal stakes. "The hardest thing about making the last movie was trying to get people to know a little bit about five major characters in the first half hour of the film," Gunn says. "It's setting up who they are. With *Vol. 2*, I've been able to crack them open so we get to know them better and in a deeper way. I love these characters like I love my own children, which I don't have. These are my children. I want the audience to get to know these characters in a way like you would get to know a friend down the line, or in the way you'd get to know somebody whom you're dating down the line. You get to explore their intricacies.

"They're all problematic individuals with a lot of psychological issues. Having flawed characters means they have to find that part of them that is unselfish, and that's the struggle of the Guardians both in the last movie and in this one in different ways. It's finding the part of themselves that's able to forgive, to find that part of themselves that is good, to find that part of themselves that is a hero. That's something we can all relate to, especially coming from such an odd group of characters—and most of us, for better or worse, think we're odd. Somewhere inside we think we don't belong, and that's who the Guardians are for and that's what they're about."

Yondu and Nebula, who saw minimal yet impactful screen time in the first film, also will have a chance to shine—and maybe even learn to become heroes themselves. "The relationship between Nebula and Gamora was portrayed as a bit one-sided in the first film," Executive Producer Victoria Alonso says. "We saw that they were sisters, but one was clearly bad and the other good. That's it. I think when we get to know their past and their relationship a little more, that's not really the case."

"I think growing up, the bully was actually Gamora—it wasn't Nebula," Gunn says. "Nebula's deep-seated resentment toward Gamora comes from a place where she loves her, and she just always wanted her older sister to love her, but she never got that. It was a cyclical pattern of being torn apart and put back together again by Thanos. It's two sisters who love each other—and for Nebula it's about accepting the fact that she loves her sister, finding where her rage comes from. And I think for Gamora it's learning to love, which I'm not sure she ever really has."

As the character-centric story unfolds, the audience accompanies the Guardians on a journey into uncharted, colorful locations that accentuate the tone of the narrative. "We've now got grounded characters we know and love, which allows us to explore some more outlandish places than we did in the first film," Gunn says.

"There's a lot out there to draw from in the comics," D'Esposito says. "There's a lot to draw from James' imagination. Seeing those two collide, I think, has been such a fun part of the process. James has drawn a lot of really fun, pulp images from his movie. It's super-colorful, the same way that movie one was."

"We're even trying to push those colors even further, and try to make them more resonant and more elegant, and try to make the world feel like those cool pulp-fiction covers from the '50s and '60s that characterized sci-fi for a long, long time," Alonso says.

Production Designer Scott Chambliss embraced the challenge inherent in such an aesthetic. "The worlds in the film are so different from each other," Chambliss says. "It's something I loved about designing

MANTIS

WES CRAIG, SERGE LAPOINTE, and NATHAN FAIRBAIRN with BRAD WALKER, ANDREW HENNESSY, and WIL QUINTANA (inset)

the film. The opportunity to create as much of a contrast as we possibly can, to set them off each other, is really exciting—tough, but definitely exciting. It was all about evolution. We knew that one world would be gold and blue, and we also already knew that the whole Ravager world was rusty, rotten factory tones and gunk. The next major piece of the evolution of what the color palette was had to do with Ego, which was the hardest to develop. It's such a unique piece that's based on something that doesn't really exist—it's been fascinating to define what it is. It was a constant process of 'What about this? What about that? Let's try this. Let's mix that up with that.' Eventually it becomes its own unique thing."

Marvel's *Guardians of the Galaxy Vol. 2* boasts an abundance of intricately designed worlds populated with unique inhabitants, but the filmmakers also faced the challenge of maintaining the sense of style and tone established in the first film. The sensational soundtrack that acts as a heartbeat to the story provided just such a connective tissue. "From a character standpoint, the music is Quill's connection to Earth—and his connection to his mother, to the life that he left behind," Schwartz says. "*Awesome Mix Vol. 2* is a big player in the movie. We saw Quill get it at the end of the first film. We heard the first track, and it really left the audience wanting more. It's integral because it highlights more than the style of the film—it plays a part in the plot."

"The discovery of each of the songs for the audience is incredibly important to us," Gunn says. "I think the songs represent whatever scene they're in very well. Sometimes they're a very accurate reflection of it, sometimes they're a counterpoint or an ironic counterpoint to what's occurring on screen. We're a big pop film that also has a lot of other elements to it, and hopefully a lot of the songs we've chosen feel the same way."

What is it, though, that makes the *Guardians* franchise so visually and tonally unique and inspired? According to Gunn, it's all about mixing genres. "I grew up loving Hong Kong films, and one of the things I loved about them was they didn't care," Gunn says. "You want to have something that's really funny in a movie? Put something really funny in there. You want to have something that's really dark? Have something really dark. Hey, let's put a dance and a singing number in the middle of the film. If people like it, why not? They really would just do whatever they had to do to entertain an audience. I don't think the Guardians are exactly like that, but I think I learned a lot from those types of films growing up and allowing myself to mix genres in a way that is hopefully very interconnected with a nice flow.

"Life isn't one thing. Life isn't just a western, life isn't just a comedy, life isn't just a drama. It's all those things. I think that's what the Guardians are. It's a more accurate reflection of our real world; it just happens to be in outer space with a talking raccoon and a talking tree who's, well, now more of a talking shrub. We really aren't trying to make anything 'better' with *Vol. 2.* I think it's a matter of allowing us to change and for people to go on this journey with these characters. Some of our characters live, some of our characters die. These are all a part of life. You never know exactly what's going to happen in this *Guardians* universe."

THE **GUARDIANS** OF THE **YEAR 3000**
ALEX ROSS

CHAPTER 1
SOVEREIGN

WELCOME TO SOVEREIGN: a planet Production Designer Scott Chambliss describes as "historic art deco design blended with the extravagantly explosive graphic punch of *Amazing Stories* magazine covers from the 1950s." Drawing inspiration from both Cecil B. DeMille's *Cleopatra* and the city of Las Vegas, Chambliss—along with Director James Gunn and their fellow filmmakers—sought to create a world that would open the film in unique fashion. Sovereign is home to the statuesque Ayesha and her gold-skinned cohorts—as well as the battery-devouring beast the Guardians find themselves battling at the onset of the film. Chambliss says that "grounding the fantasy culture in something accessible but not necessarily expected" was the greatest challenge in breathing life into the planet.

"We're building these cultures from the ground up and telling the audience what they're about before anyone ever says a word," Executive Producer Jonathan Schwartz says. "James and Scott had a very distinct vision for what they wanted to do. This movie is a huge challenge from a design perspective, because we go to so many specific worlds. We never want to feel like we're floating to a world that's solely made up for the purposes of science fiction. There's a roundedness and grittiness to the life of *Guardians of the Galaxy*, which makes it fly off the screen. Sovereign is an excellent example of that. Scott was really able to infuse the movie in a great way with reality and with life."

SELLARS

STAR-LORD

Revisiting Peter Quill's look wasn't so much about reinventing the wheel, but rather embracing a simple, natural evolution of the character, Visual Development Supervisor Andy Park says. "In the beginning of the project, James expressed that he was quite happy with the way the main characters from the first film looked and wasn't looking to revamp them in any major way. He didn't want to create a team look like in the comics. Even though they're a family, they're also individuals. He wanted us to explore a more relaxed look. Star-Lord is no longer a Ravager, but has come to identify himself with his signature long and short jackets. So this was a case where exploring looks was more about how to show his evolution from where he was in the first film to where he is now. He's saved the universe, is famous, and is part of a team that he considers his family—albeit a dysfunctional family. I gave a slightly updated look to his jacket, and a bit of a less piecemeal look. And I tried giving him accessories such as a scarf, necklaces, a T-shirt, and a gauntlet that expresses how he sees himself as confident, in control, and a rock star. Besides those looks, I had to also explore some looks with the signature blue."

PARK

STAR-LORD'S COMMUNICATOR

EAVES

PARK

SZE

CORDELLA

FUENTEBELLA

AERO RIGS

"The Aero Rigs had to feel equally iconic and heroic, as well as fit with all the characters from Rocket to Gamora and not feel out of place," Visual Development Illustrator Rodney Fuentebella says. "I wanted them to feel in the same technologic world as Star-Lord's helmet. I created a lot of different looks playing with different shapes, sizes, and configurations of mechanical elements to figure out what would work best not only in look, but also in practicality. James Gunn offered a lot of great feedback in order to hone in on a final design. We worked with Legacy Effects to realize my design in 3-D and eventually fabricate them as tangible, wearable pieces."

CORDELLA and FUENTEBELLA

PARK

GAMORA

As with Star-Lord, Gamora's new look was about establishing attitude and personality, a major visual leap for the character. "Gamora was another costume where James wanted it more grounded," Costume Designer Judianna Makovsky says. "I started by working with Andy [Park], who delivered an initial, beautiful design. And while there were some 'making' issues, the essence, the concept was there. So we set out to turn it into a costume.

Zoe [Saldana] actually came in with some good ideas about having the T-shirt cut up, sort of like a 'punk rock band' look. For the coat, I wanted something simple, nothing outrageous. The stitching and seaming creates a very '80s look, which James loved. But her costume is really just a vest and leather pants—very grounded, very non-'super hero'—exactly what James asked us to do."

"Gamora is no longer the warrior assassin for Thanos," Andy Park says. "She's now her own person who found a purpose and a family in the Guardians of the Galaxy. I explored only a couple warrior-type looks. It was a fine balance because she is still one of the greatest warriors in the galaxy, but I wanted to create a softer look for her. So like Star-Lord, I explored materials that are less traditionally 'super hero'—things like tank tops, jackets, various accessories, and the like. I was trying to find a look that conveyed her individuality, her confidence, and still with a touch of her warrior spirit."

EAVES

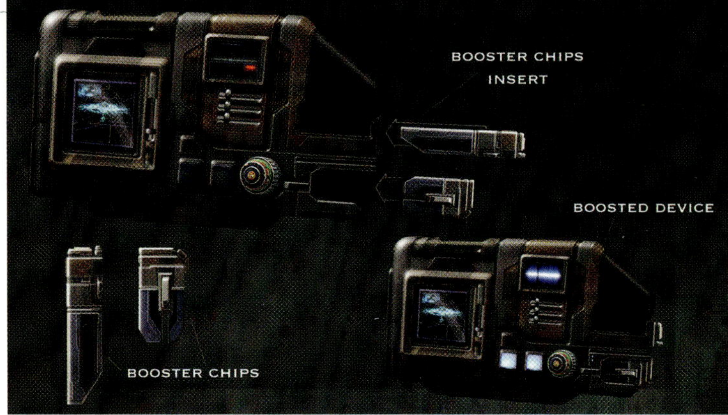

PARK

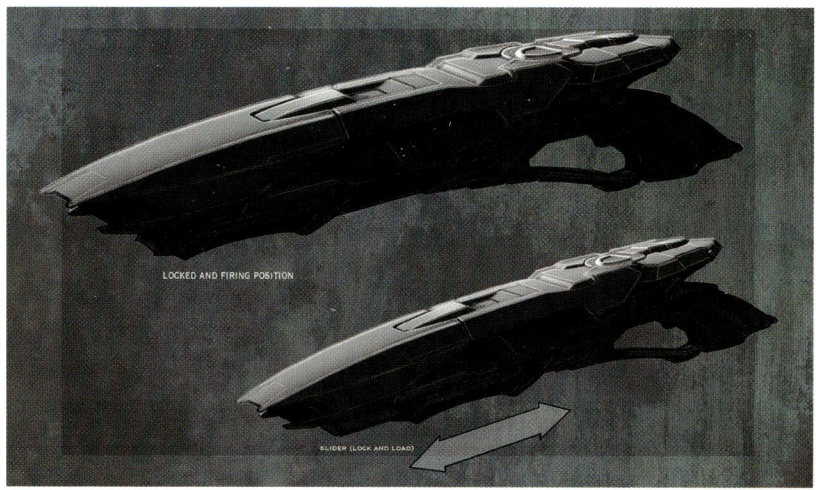

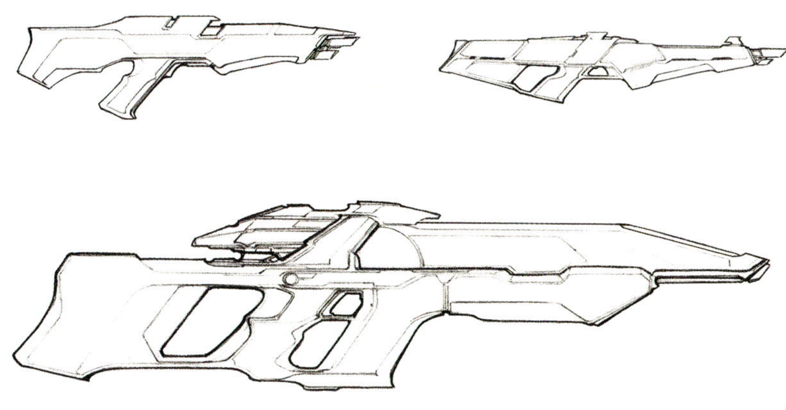

EAVES

Guardians of Galaxy Vol. 2 represents Prop Illustrator John Eaves' eighth film working with Prop Master Russell Bobbitt. "He had me start drawing a gaggle of different weapons, mostly rifles with all kinds of heavy and multiple-barrel configurations," Eaves says. "Once we had about 30 concepts, the producers and director all came down and went through Russell's labyrinth of toys and ideas. This happens quickly, and by the time we are going down the line of designs, things will get shifted from one table to another. For example, what was put out to be for Yondu sometimes will work better for Gamora. Adding to her usual weapon of choice, her sword, we added a pretty heavy rifle for her to use. Two variations were created both with over and under firing systems, and a targeting scope. Everything that we would design would have a weathered finish."

PARK

PARK

CORDELLA

CORDELLA

DRAX

As seen in the first film, Drax doesn't believe in clothes. Couple that with the iconography of the tattoos covering his upper body, and the result is a character who didn't require a revamp. The process of transforming actor Dave Bautista into Drax did get an overhaul, though. "His makeup on the first movie was wonderful, but it took five hours to put on," James Gunn says. "This time around, they were able to do it in under two hours. It's a big difference in the look, because it looks much better. It much more tightly adheres to his skin. The last skin got very wrinkly, but that's part of it. It was also better because Dave would come to set way more awake. Coming to set after five hours of makeup versus coming to set two hours after makeup—especially when you have to hang from rigs and do fight scenes for 12 hours straight—can be very difficult. I think that our makeup team at Legacy Effects really came through to recreate this makeup in a way that was more user-friendly."

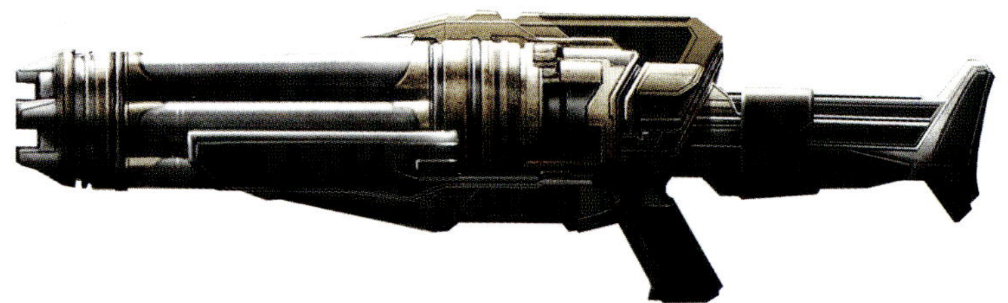

CORDELLA

EAVES

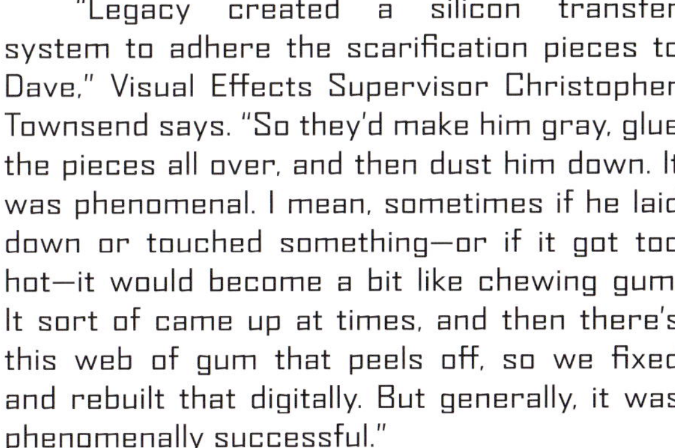

"Legacy created a silicon transfer system to adhere the scarification pieces to Dave," Visual Effects Supervisor Christopher Townsend says. "So they'd make him gray, glue the pieces all over, and then dust him down. It was phenomenal. I mean, sometimes if he laid down or touched something—or if it got too hot—it would become a bit like chewing gum. It sort of came up at times, and then there's this web of gum that peels off, so we fixed and rebuilt that digitally. But generally, it was phenomenally successful."

KUTSCHE

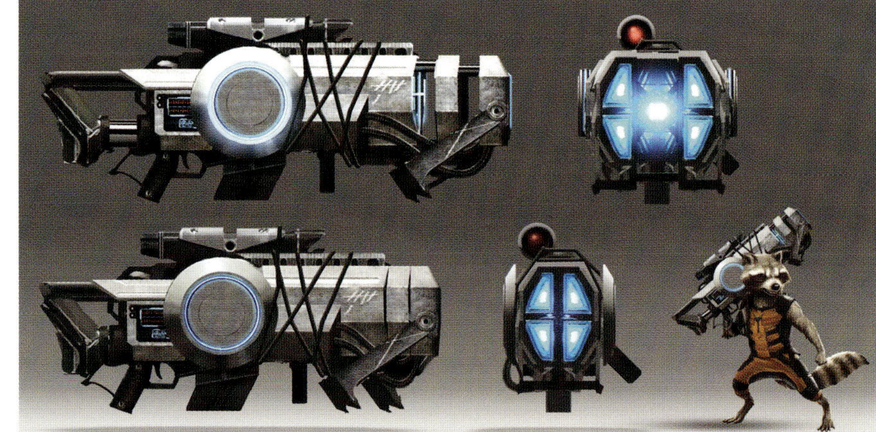

METHOD STUDIOS

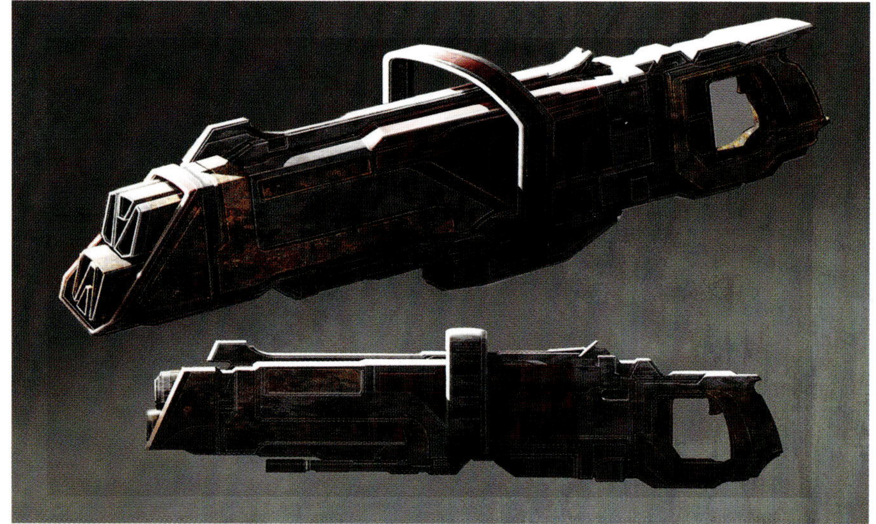

EAVES

ROCKET

Like most of the other Guardians, fast-talking, gun-toting Rocket received a costume makeover. "The underlying direction for the Guardians this time around was to make them more 'rock 'n' roll,'" Visual Development Illustrator Jackson Sze says. "Knowing that, I took inspiration from classic rock stars—with torn sleeves, leather wear, intricate jewelry, etc." Sze experimented with various designs, keeping in mind the spirit and nuances of the character.

SZE

DIAZ

"Rocket is always tinkering with equipment, building gadgets and powerful guns. I made sure to include functionality in his look so he has access to the tools he'll need. Even though Rocket has to take care of Baby Groot, he is still a tough mercenary at heart, always ready for danger. Functional suits and advanced weaponry will still be at the core of Rocket's look. The cybernetic implants from his past are still there, but they do not dictate his look."

SZE

EAVES

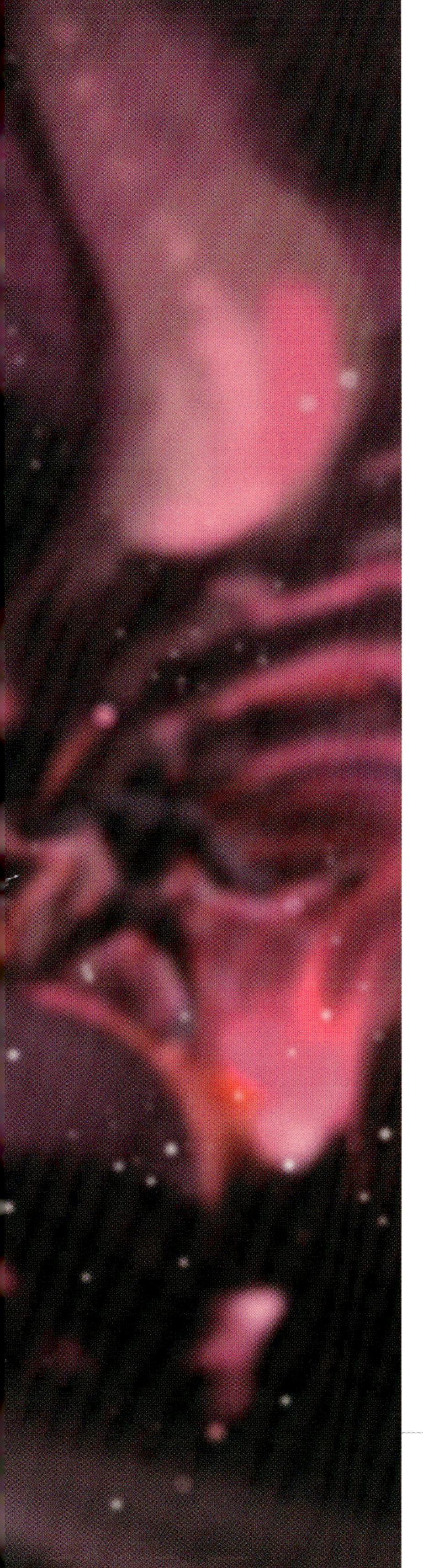

FRANCISCO

GROOT

Visual Development Illustrator Anthony Francisco, who designed the initial iteration of Baby Groot for the first film's finale, was tasked with further fleshing out the character to give him even more personality and life. "James Gunn's direction was pretty clear from the beginning," Francisco says. "For the first film, James wanted him to be in a pot and almost just like a stick with a face. I had done some really rough ideas trying to get a range from cute to really weird, but trying to keep in mind the direction I was given. For *Guardians Vol. 2*, Andy Park had told me that they wanted to see Baby Groot out of his pot...and dancing!

FRANCISCO

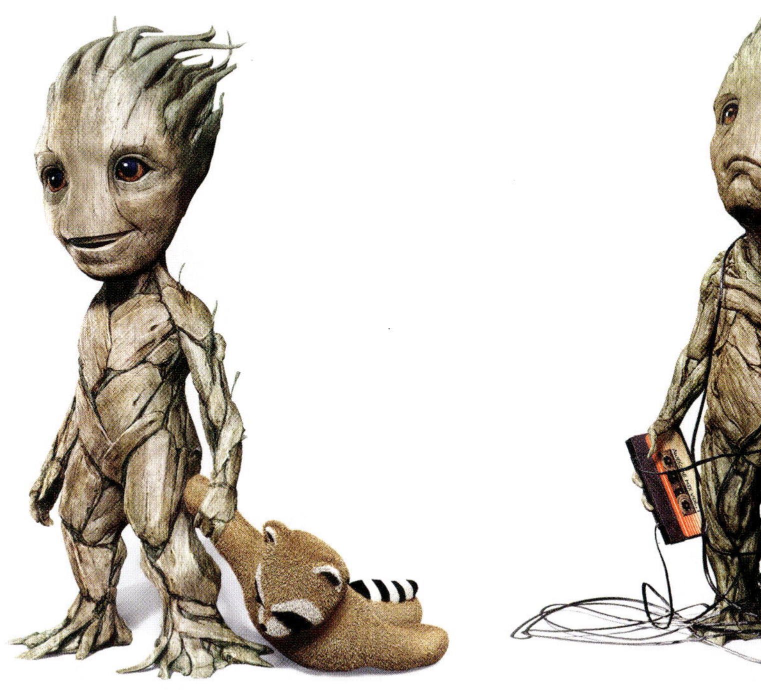

HERMAN

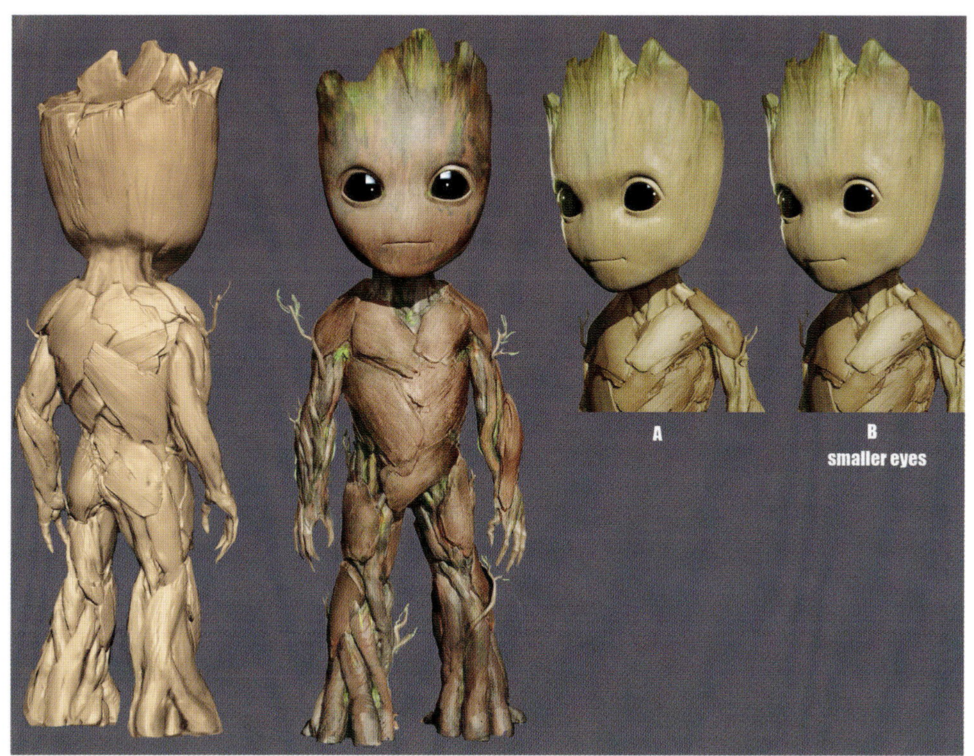

FRANCISCO

FRANCISCO

"I had the perfect reference," Francisco says. "My son and daughter love to dance, and became my inspiration when I started designing. I pretty much copied their proportions, specifically my four-year-old son's way of standing and his expressions. It felt appropriate, seeing as how *Guardians Vol. 2* is all about heart and family, using my kids as inspiration. They offered a lot of personality and emotion to help breathe life into my designs."

DIAZ and FRANCISCO

METHOD STUDIOS

SELLARS

SOVEREIGN

The Sovereign world's bold design elements were born from the self-indulgent personality of its populace. "Ayesha and her culture are theoretically perfect and beautiful in every conceivable way, a self-perception that leads them into self-obsessed obliviousness," Scott Chambliss says. "In short, they're gorgeous, garish airheads. They also have breathtakingly gaudy taste."

"We were terrified that it was going to look like a Las Vegas show," Judianna Makovsky says. "It couldn't be sequin-y, shiny gold. James suggested that the civilization was an older civilization, so we went with very old golds. There is a bit of shine to things, but it's simple.

"I wanted the citizens of Sovereign to stay away from anything that felt too renaissance or too medieval. James Gunn is very rooted in the '80s, citing movies like *Flash Gordon* as reference. We kept the designs simple, with a splash of modern, with touches of bronze and navy blue."

SELLARS

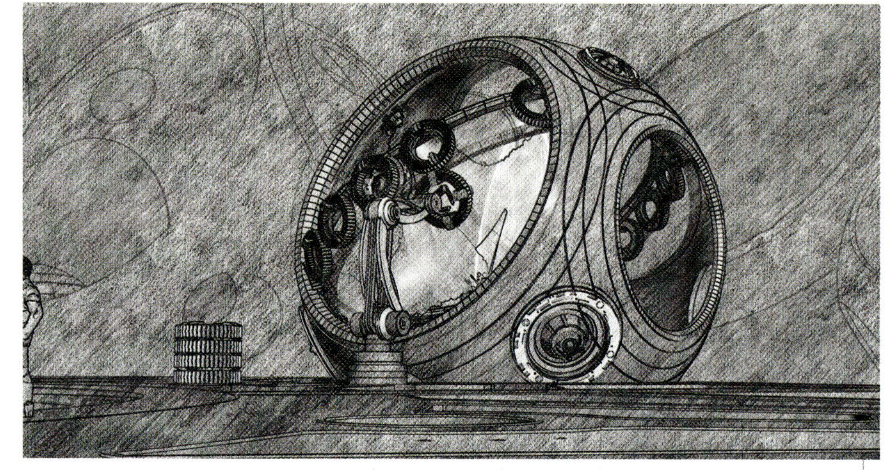

NOWAK

previous SELLARS, NOWAK and MCFADYEN

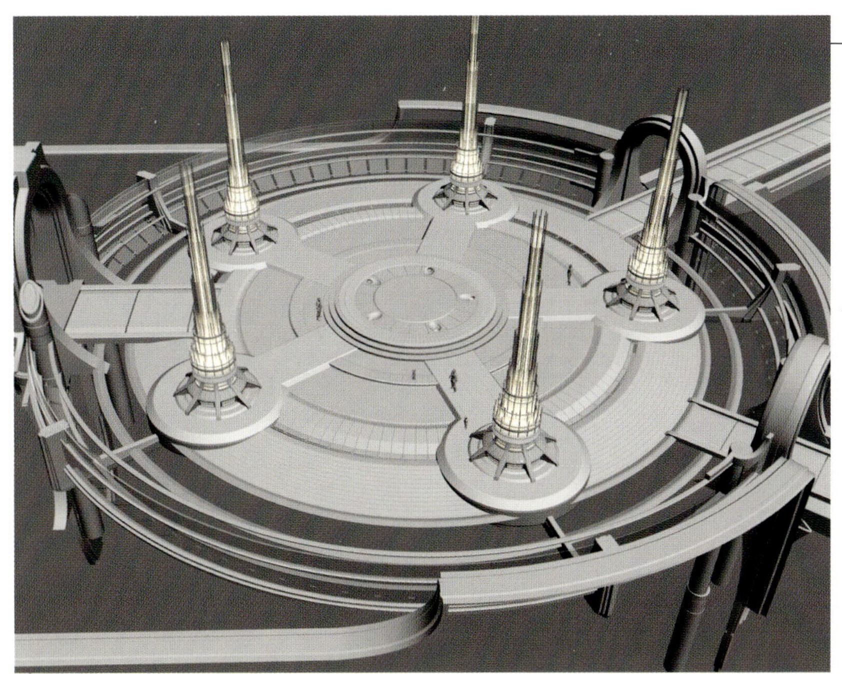

THE ANULAX BATTERIES

The Anulax Batteries are a hot commodity: An interdimensional monster wants to eat them, the Guardians are trying to protect them, and Nebula is out to steal them. Rocket helps himself to some of the batteries, inciting a Sovereign retaliation: High priestess Ayesha hires Yondu and his Ravagers to track down the Guardians, kill them, and retrieve the batteries. The inspiration for the sought-after technology was decidedly mundane, Scott Chambliss says. "The precious batteries that power the Sovereign were based on big, clunky 1930s microphones."

NOWAK

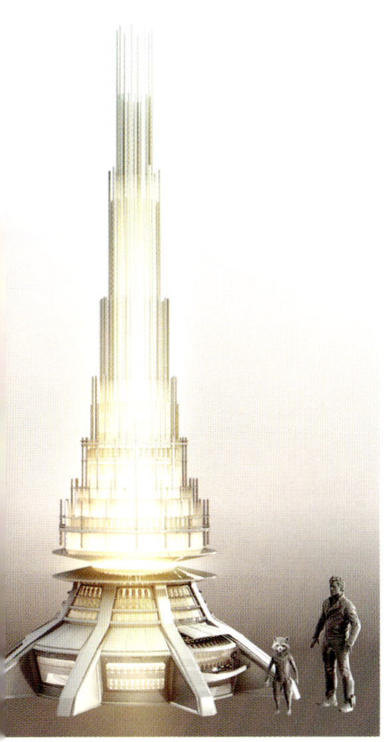

NOWAK

"This keyframe was meant to convey several things," Andy Park says. "It is the intro to the film; it depicts the team as just that, a team; and of course it introduces the audience to the adorable and naive Baby Groot and his free-spirited personality. The Guardians of the Galaxy are now rock stars in the universe and are hired by the Sovereign to protect them from an energy-eating interdimensional beast, the Abilisk. Baby Groot hears music and inevitably dances in the foreground, oblivious to the danger behind him. It's got to be one of the best intros to a film ever."

FRANCISCO

PARK

ABILISK

The unsightly Abilisk is a fearsome beast whose appetite for Anulax Batteries leads to an epic showdown with the Guardians. "I knew I didn't want to give him legs, because you wouldn't really need legs when you're coasting through space," Anthony Francisco says. "Initially, I was thinking that it could propel itself through space with strategically placed openings to push air out, much like an octopus. This is another one of those creatures where James was clear with his direction. He wanted a creature with tentacles, but with the texture of a hairless mole rat.

When I think of aliens, the first thing that comes to mind is sea creatures. I think they are the best in terms of initial research, and just through my experience in designing aliens. There are so many concepts of their natural design that you can use; they are just so weird. I personally think of creature design in percentages of ingredients that I mix into a magical pot and simmer. For the Abilisk, it was 70 percent octopus elements, but with a rib cage, and 25 percent my centerpiece, which is the teeth inspired from a lamprey—and five percent is the texture/color of a hairless mole rat. I thought of it as a shark, but in space—all you see is teeth, and everything about its design is to get those teeth to the source of food as efficiently as possible. I know it's a simple idea, but sometimes simplicity is the key to a clear design."

MARANTZ

HIGH PRIESTESS AYESHA

The Sovereign leader, Ayesha, is decadently outfitted and imposingly beautiful. "We needed to establish Ayesha's look first, as she's the figurehead of the Sovereign race; her look was bound to inform the rest of the world," Judianna Makovsky says. "Height was a major part of the design. Elizabeth [Debicki], the actress playing her, was so tall—and we wanted to make her even taller. We wanted her to tower

CHEN

previous PARK

over Peter Quill and the others. She ended up being about six foot seven by the time we were done with her platform shoes. Aside from height, establishing the overall proportions was challenging. We wanted her to be beautiful, regal, respected—like people would actually like her. There's also a level of sensuality to her: We wanted to see the shape of her body while also making it look like she was covered in metal—but metal and soft at the same time. Getting the makeup to read as the same tone as the clothes and have her fit into a specific part of her throne—it was a very collaborative process."

SELLARS and CHEN

CHEN

The throne room mixes dark navy with gold—the sort of stark visual contrast evident in multiple locations throughout the film. Fastened in at the headpiece, Ayesha appears to be part of the sprawling throne. "Designing the headpiece was extremely tough," Makovsky says. "Headpieces can minimize head size—or conversely, feel clunky and awkward. It needed to fit her like the rest of her costume, offering overall shape and structure. It was a lot of research and development to find the right look."

CHEN

SHIH and CHEN

SHIH

SHIH

SWEET

SWEET

SHIH

CHEN

CHEN

CHEN

AYESHA'S THRONE ROOM

SELLARS

AYESHA'S HANDMAIDENS

Ayesha is flanked by a group of equally imposing handmaidens. "The handmaidens were all at least six feet tall," Judianna Makovsky says. "With the shoes we put them in, they were about six foot five. Their costumes were far more simplistic than Ayesha's, but I used shapes that were reminiscent of Ayesha's look. They're all in the same world. Their headpieces were based off old '20s and '30s silent movies."

SOVEREIGN'S CITIZENS

SHIH

BOUTTE

NEBULA

Last seen commandeering a Ravager airship after cutting off her own cybernetic hand to escape Gamora, Nebula begins the film as a prisoner of the Sovereign. "I think Nebula has only changed from the first film in that at the end of the first movie, we see Nebula very distinctly decide that everyone around her is crazy," James Gunn says. "She detaches herself from it all, and we find her a couple months later after the events of the first movie. Life has not been good to her. She has this crappy claw hand in replacement of her hand that she cut off in the first film. Her clothes are in tatters. In a way, she's a teen, somebody who's just moving away from home. She's a little bit rebellious and surly—unnecessarily surly at times—but I think that's all a protection for something that she has here that's a little softer than that."`

"Nebula was definitely my favorite character to concept-design in the first *Guardians of the Galaxy* film," Andy Park says. "In this story, only a couple months have passed. I did a few takes on her tattered-up costume she was already wearing, as well as a new hand—or a very rudimentary claw, in this case, due to her chopping off her hand during her fight with Gamora in the first film. I was then able to explore designing what her new hand, given to her by the Ravagers, would look like. I wanted there to be a clear feeling of an upgrade with the new hand, something that felt possibly even more high-tech than her arm. Later in the film, Nebula is outfitted in a Ravager costume that Judianna [Makovsky] and her team designed."

CORDELLA

NEBULA'S ARM

PARK

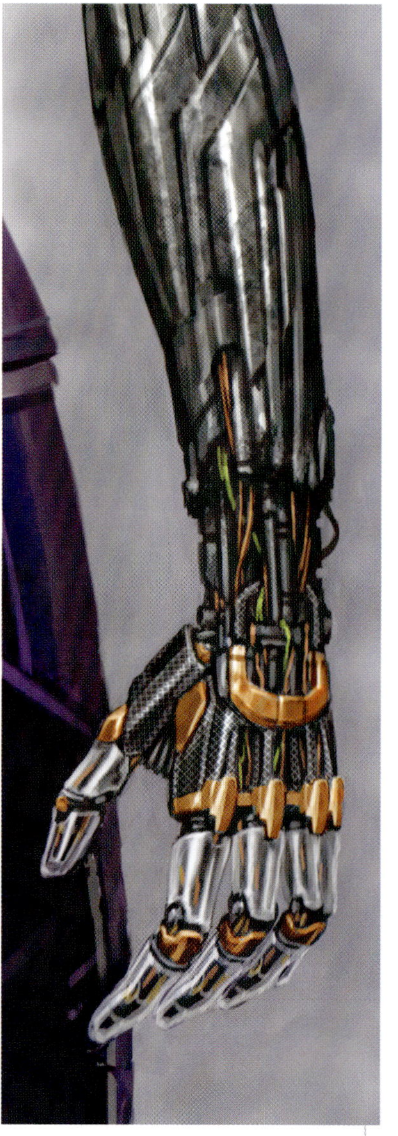

PARK

CORDELLA

NOWAK

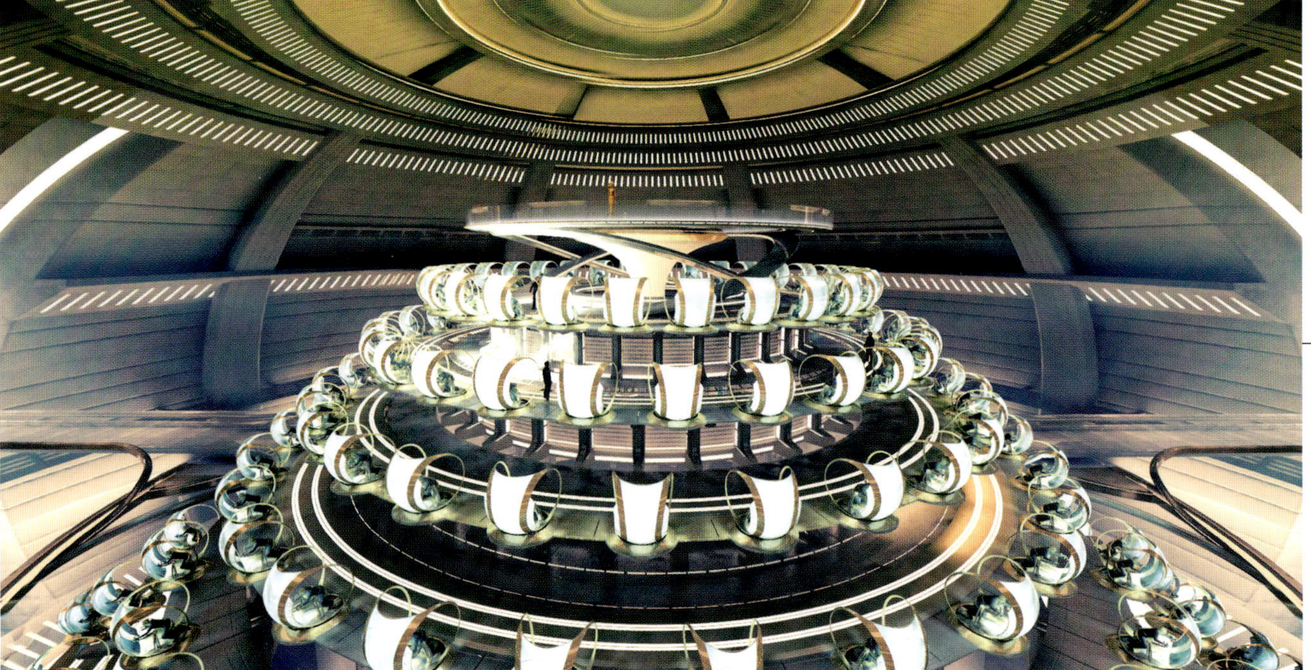

SOVEREIGN'S SPACE PODS

NOWAK

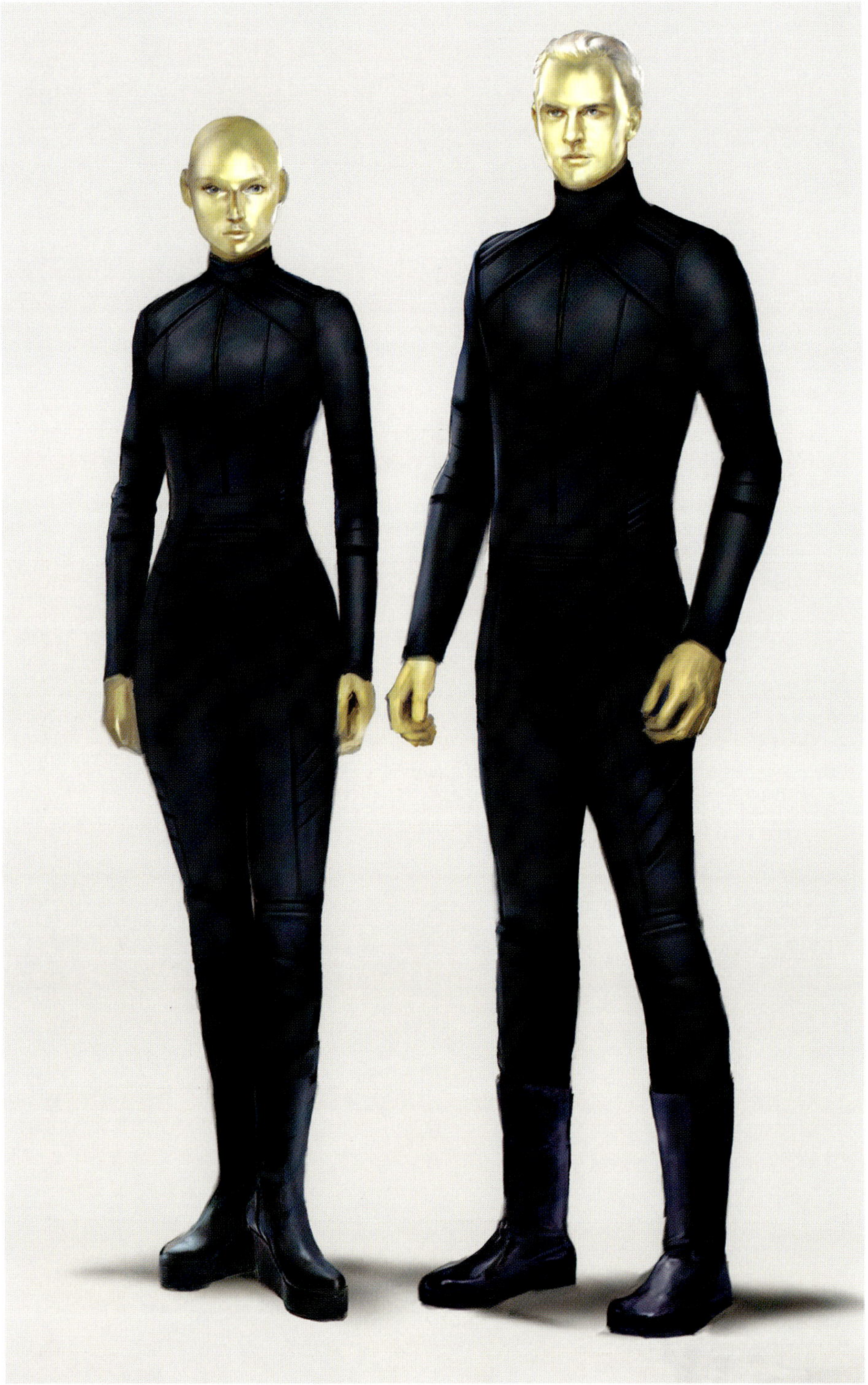

SHIH

SOVEREIGN PILOTS

"James was extremely specific with the pilots, much like he was with the citizens of Sovereign," Judianna Makovsky says. "He wanted the suits streamlined and simple—no patches or insignias, just tight-fitting, practical suits. We actually explored quite a few different looks in the beginning, but it was all too much. Working with James is great in that way: His direction is informative, and he knows exactly what he wants—especially when it comes to color. The functionality of the pilots, their placement in the pods—that was the more important part of their design. The clothes didn't need to be distracting—they needed to accentuate the action of the character."

DIAZ

KUTSCHE

HERMAN

FUENTEBELLA

ENVOYS

"The interesting design challenge creating the Envoy robots was combining the pulp idea with the aesthetics of the Sovereign, as well as keeping in mind the soldier aspect of their function," Rodney Fuentebella says. "The design shapes and body types were an open sandbox, although James cited early on that having the pilot's face visible in some type of screen would be an interesting element to add—not necessarily having a physical pilot inside the robot, but piloting it remotely somewhere else on Sovereign. I wanted to have them look functional while paying homage to the silhouettes of B-movie alien robots. Working on the Envoys was a lot more exploratory than previous mech designs, such as Iron Man, seen in the Marvel Cinematic Universe. They were quirky and full of personality."

FUENTEBELLA

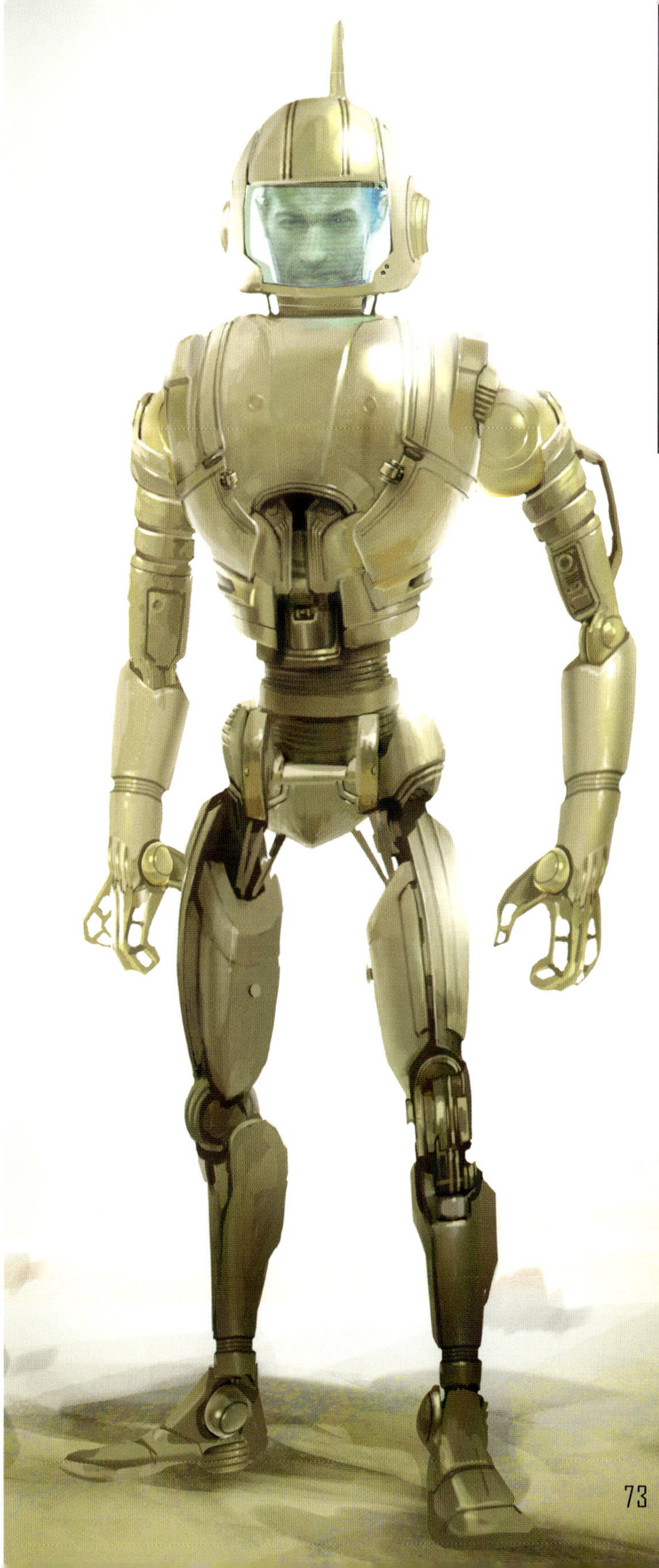

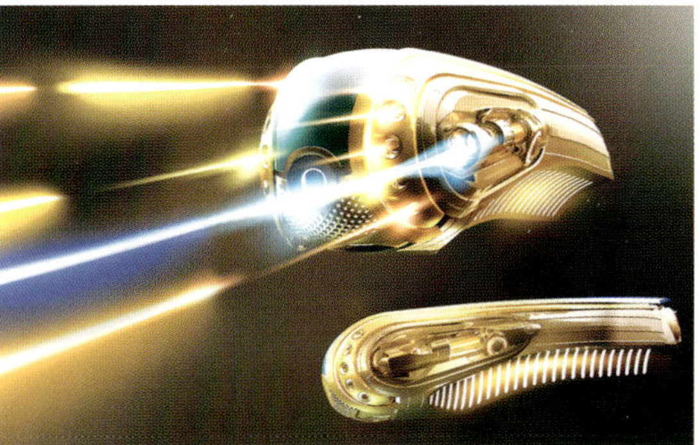

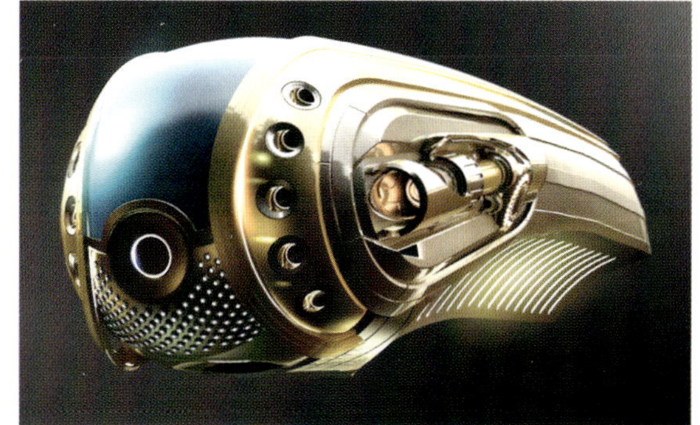

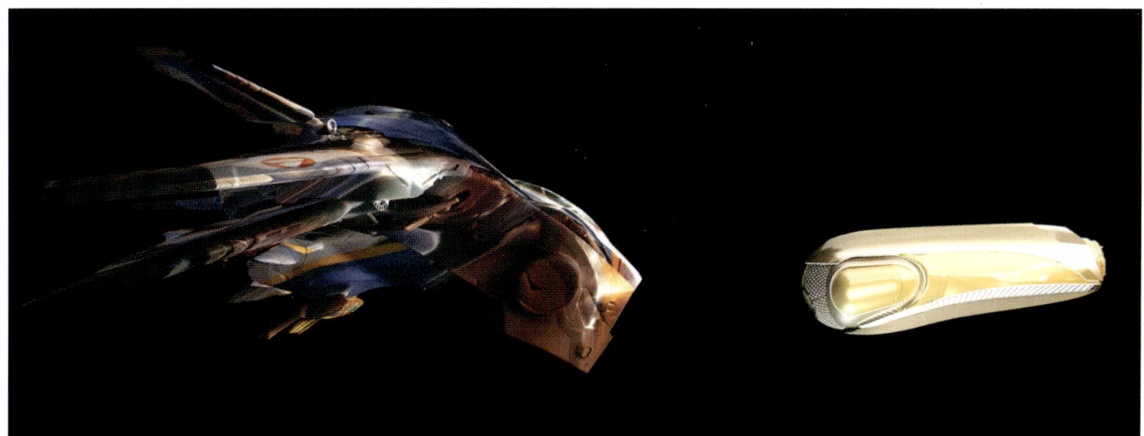

SOVEREIGN SHIPS

"Aside from the already-established ships from the previous film—the Milano and Eclector—we were attempting to create very atypical ships," Scott Chambliss says. "Who wants to see a spaceship that reminds you of five other spaceship designs you've seen?

It also helped that James Gunn seemed to be obsessed by circular shapes on this movie."

"The Sovereign have a very precise idea of beauty, and they display it proudly," Rodney Fuentebella says. "I wanted to make sure that idea of beauty is first and foremost. Taking from what the Art Department did on the base design, I was tasked to create the look of the transformed, battle-ready version."

NOWAK

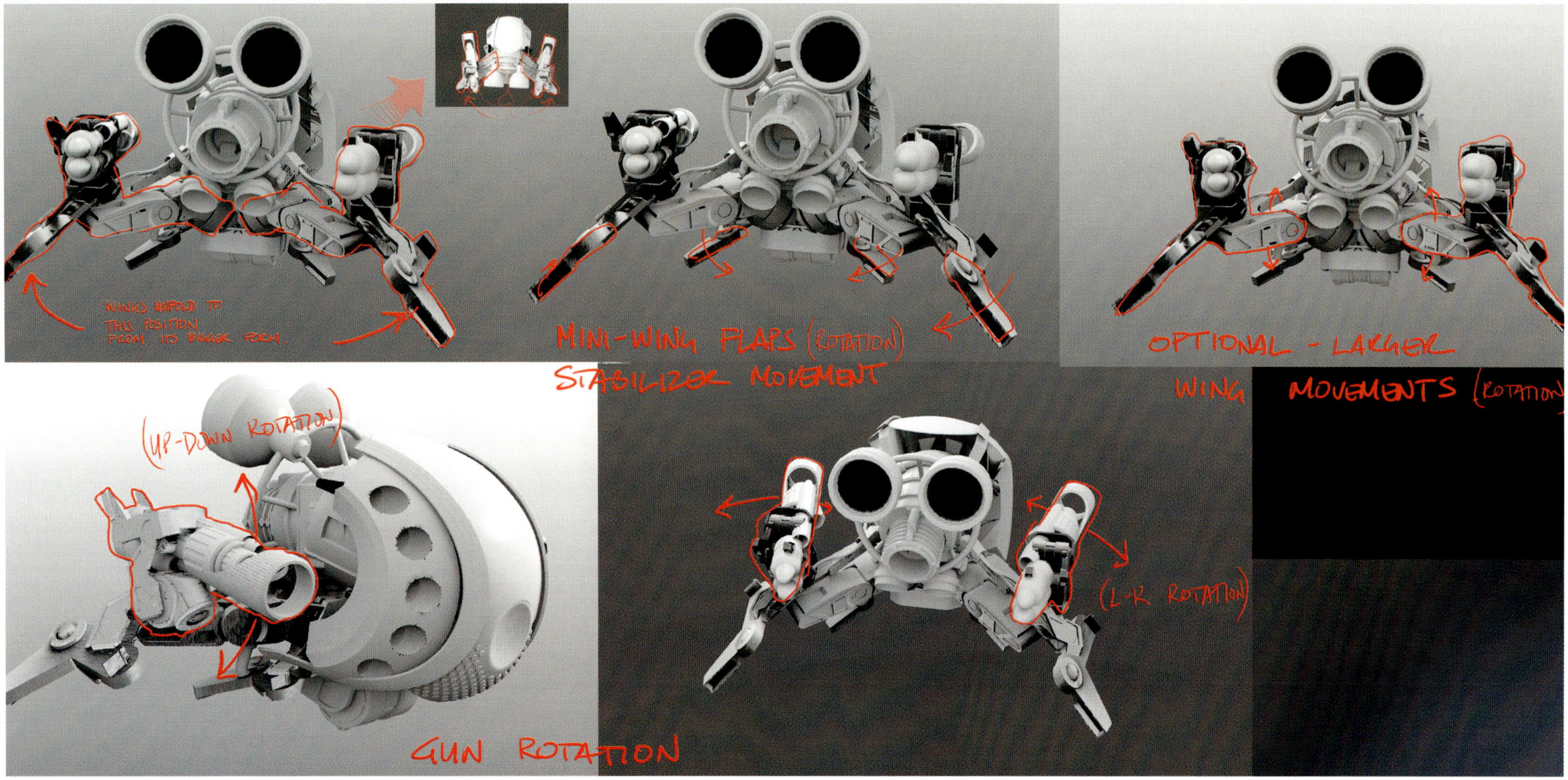

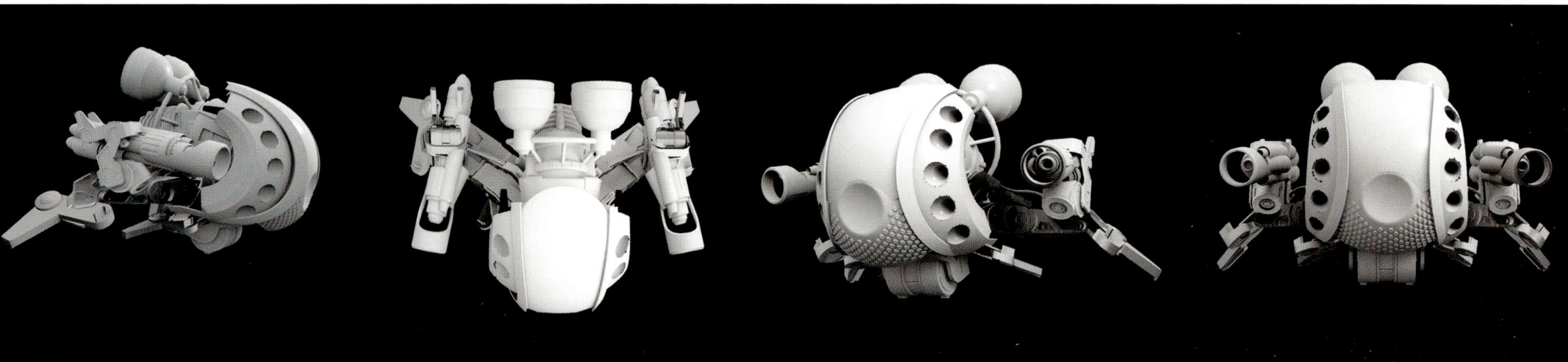

FUENTEBELLA and NOWAK

CHAPTER 2
BERHERT

WELCOME TO BERHERT: a vibrantly lush, deceptively dangerous world where the *Milano* crash-lands—stranding the team among towering trees and overgrowth. Fractured in the wake of earlier events, the Guardians are ambushed by Yondu and his Ravagers, hunting them on behalf of Ayesha and the Sovereign. "We filled a huge stage with a huge forest, and it was one of our few full 360-degree sets," Production Designer Scott Chambliss says. "There were vertical [digital] extensions, of course, but the indoor forest with a hundred huge tree trunks was quite something... after a while of shooting, so was the moldy smell."

"We always like to take it as far as we can practically," Executive Producer Jonathan Schwartz says. "There's of course a limit to how much you can do with that given that this movie is set in outer space, and has a ton of crazy space aliens and a talking raccoon and a talking tree. That said, on movie one, we had a ton of practical work—practical aliens, practical explosions, practical fights—and we've repeated that same model on movie two. Berhert is an excellent example of that mindset and execution, same with the 360 interiors of the *Eclector*."

Of the film's many fantastic locations—Sovereign, Ego, Contraxia—Berhert is the most Earth-like, with relatable textures and materials. But hints of the unusual allowed Berhert to have its own unique ecosystem. "We added a tiny bit of otherworldly, mossy, Q-tip-shaped growths dotting the landscape for good measure," Chambliss says. "It couldn't feel too much like Earth."

FUENTEBELLA

METHOD STUDIOS

"The Berhert set was mostly practical—the trees were about 25 to 35 feet tall—but the trees you see in the film are about 40 or 50 feet tall," Visual Effects Supervisor Christopher Townsend says. "We didn't have stages that tall. So the set was constructed with cut-off trees, and we extended the treetops digitally in postproduction. We also added a few trees where we couldn't physically have trees on the set to make room for camera movements—or if there was a place that felt sparse, we introduced some digital trees to fill in the space. We added additional foliage and atmosphere, such as falling leaves and branches. It's always great to have a basis of reality that we can hold on to as we introduce all of the CG elements."

DOPASO

previous SZE

METHOD STUDIOS

DOPASO

EAVES

TRIXTER

TRIXTER

REEDER

EGO'S SHIP

DOPASO

REEDER

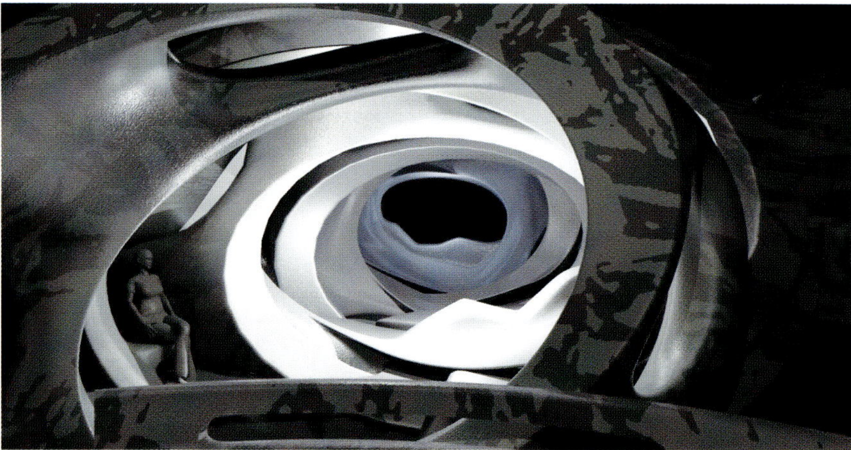

HARGREAVES

"Ego is an intergalactic adventurer in his own way who's gone to many, many different worlds and many different planets," Jonathan Schwartz says. "He has had his own kinds of adventures, not dissimilar to what the Guardians have gone through." And much like the *Milano*, Ego's ship reflects the personality of its pilot. Ego's world is organic and free-flowing, largely constructed by Ego himself. His simplistic, egg-shaped vessel embodies a similar dynamic.

"This is another example of James' affinity for cylindrical shapes in this film," Scott Chambliss says. "We knew the Sovereign ships were going to have a cylindrical silhouette, so I was keen to make sure Ego's ship didn't feel the same. We went through a number of designs; as the look of Ego evolved, his ship evolved, too. Once Ego's design was finalized, as well as his planet, his ship naturally took shape."

METHOD STUDIOS

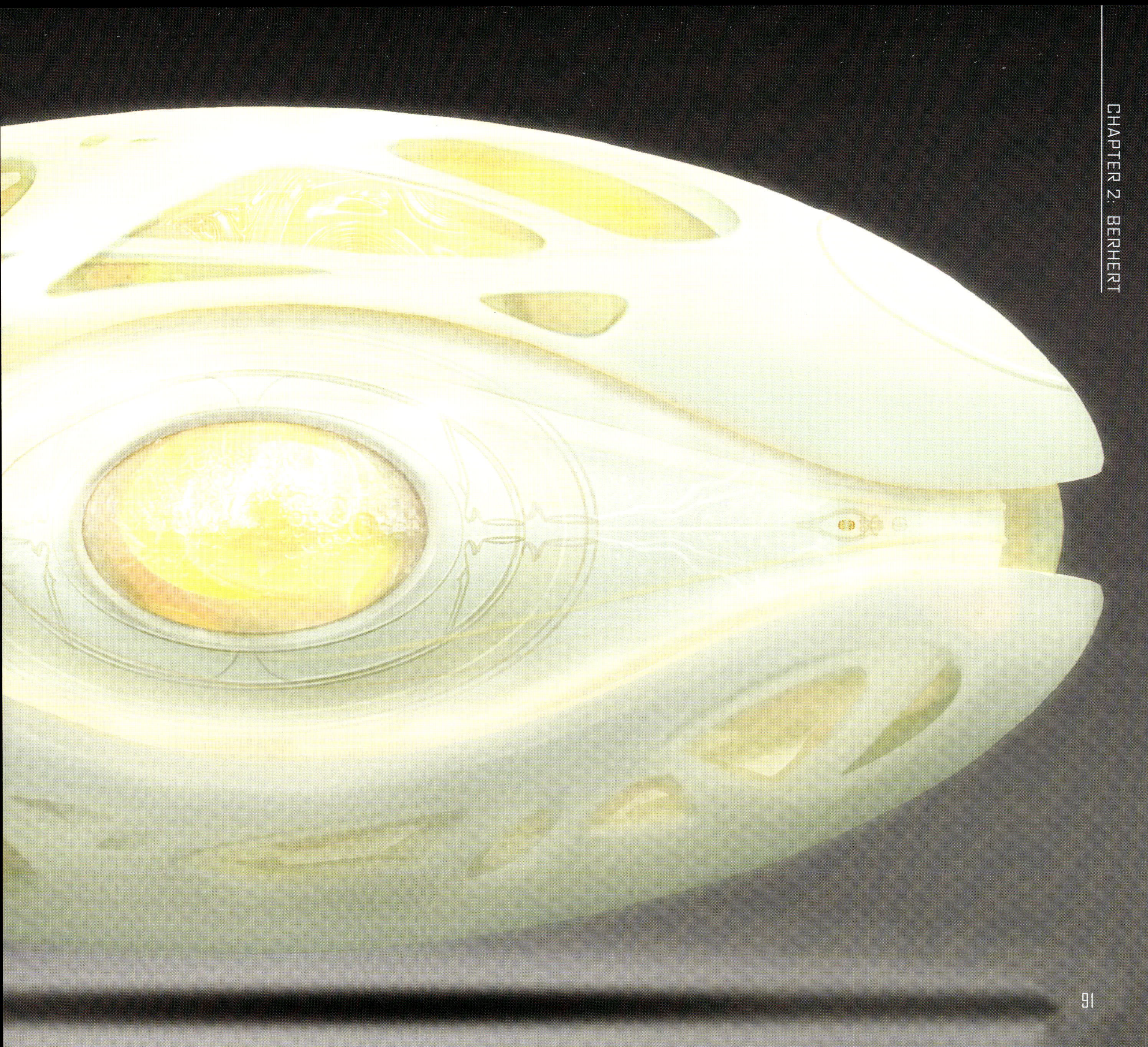

EGO

A mysterious man in an organic spaceship arrives on Berhert and emerges from the high-tech vessel with unmatched swagger, exuding a confidence reminiscent of our heroic lead, Peter Quill. Coincidence? Not at all. Ego is Quill's father, a character as complex as the design process required to conceptualize his look in the film. "Ego was by far the most challenging character to design," Visual Development Supervisor Andy Park says. "I, along with the rest the Visual Development team, tackled looks that ran the visual gamut. The design process lasted all the way up until just weeks before shooting began. He is the pivotal character in this film, and finding his look was central to so many other aspects of the production. He's a unique character because he's also the planet he lives on. So there definitely had to be a unity in his look with the environment, ships, and architecture of his world. And as the production designer [Scott Chambliss] explored what the world would look like, it would affect how we approached his look, and vice versa. It was a unique challenge. We tackled looks that had more of a 'swashbuckling pirate' to a 'gunslinging cowboy' feel, to more 'organic earthy' looks—all the while trying to maintain the 'pulpy sci-fi' look James wanted to have. There were certain points in the production where a look was settled on, and then later it was decided that it wasn't right for different reasons. The final design was beautifully executed by Jackson Sze."

SZE

SZE

FRANCISCO

"For the audience to see and understand Ego as Quill's father, he had to be strong and charismatic," Jackson Sze says. "The fact that he is also a planet, and an explorer of new frontiers, had to be factored into his look, as well. We were discovering Ego along with James. Character notes were

SZE

updated frequently, so our designs had to reflect this dynamic—resulting in lots and lots of designs. We tried clothing made of and grown by his planet, then looks that invoke a glamorous space rock star. Also, we took stabs at frontier space cowboys and iconic classic sci-fi suits. All the while, Ego's own planet was coming into clearer and clearer focus from the Art Department—which helped us understand Ego's environment, as well. Toward the end, a few ideas and visuals that James liked through the design process carried over in other iterations. The 'frontier space cowboy' look evolved with elements of his planet's form language. An attitude and space-weariness was captured, resulting in a design that hopefully speaks to Ego's travels and origin. To have Kurt Russell play this character just made his look that much more compelling, grounded with warmth and humanity."

"Kurt Russell is a naturally likable guy," Director James Gunn says. "He told me a story about when he was about to shoot *Escape from New York*, which was one of my favorite movies as a kid. The studio heads were reading the script, and they're going, 'This character is completely unlikable. Why are we going to care about this movie?' Kurt replied, 'Because he's played by me, and I'm just a naturally likable guy.' That's exactly who he is, both in person and on screen. I think that is something that was necessary for Ego to come in, and the character does have an ego. Chris Pratt and I have talked about this from the very inception of the idea: It's about our egos. It's about the fact that we made a movie that was so successful, and trying to stay down to earth and remain who we are as human beings—and not letting the ego side take over, because it can ruin a person's life. So, yes, this movie is about a father and a son. But it's also really autobiographical about me and Chris and Zoe and Dave, who have been through this journey together and are now going to the next step."

FRANCISCO

CORDELLA

FRANCISCO

HERMAN

CHEN

SZE

PARK

FUENTEBELLA

FUENTEBELLA

SZE

FRANCISCO

SZE

FRANCISCO

SZE

FRANCISCO

PARK

PARK

PARK

MANTIS

The empathic alien Mantis is Ego's right hand. "The advantage of working on a *Guardians of the Galaxy* film is that the characters are all relatively unknown," Andy Park says. "So there's a freedom in approaching their look and feel. We're not as beholden to their comic-book counterparts as we are with our other films. Mantis was a character James wanted to bring into the roster from the very outset of production. Oftentimes when we work on designing a character, we don't get much information on what to explore. With Mantis, James knew three things from the get-go: one, he wanted to cast an Asian actress; two, he wanted us to explore the insectoid aspect of the character; and three, he didn't want her to be green like in the comic books (for obvious reasons: Gamora). I explored a variety of designs staying in a range that kept her attractive, yet obviously alien and with varying degrees of insect-like qualities. As usual, I always refer heavily on the comic-book source material. I know there's at least one hardcore Mantis fan out there, so I have to respect her roots."

PARK

PARK

PARK

PARK

"If you talk to any artist, he/she will tell you that during their school years, they would always doodle along the margins of their paper during class," Andy Park says. "Well, early in the pre-production stage of this film, I had a story meeting with James and several other crew members, and during that meeting I did what I do best: I doodled. Specifically, there was talk about Mantis and her role in the film. So while the brainstorming and discussion went on, I sketched out some thoughts I had on Mantis. Some of my best ideas are found in the margins of lined paper or on Post-it notes."

PARK

PARK

LEGACY EFFECTS

TRIXTER

FOLLOWING CHART SHOWS A REPRESENTATION OF CHANGE IN THE TIP-GLOW, DEPENDING ON HER EMOTIONS.

THE MID-POINT EQUALS AN IDLE STATE (ALMOST) NO GLOW AND NO VARIATION IN FREQUENZY. THE INTENSER MANTIS EMOTION GET THE HIGHER THE FREQUENCY GETS. IF MANTIS EXPERIENCES EXTREME HAPPIENESS OR ANGER FOR EXAMPLE, THE TIPS START BLINKING FASTER WITH AN INCREASING INTENSITY SUPPORTED BY THE ACTRESS' PERFORMANCE THIS SHOULD SERVE ENOUGH INFORMATION FOR THE VIEWER TO INTERPRETE HER EMOTION - WITHOUT CHANGING THE ACTUAL COLOR OF THE TIP.

ADDITIONALY THE "TIP-FEATHERS" COULD VARY IN MOVEMENT AS WELL. ANGRY BEEING A CLOSED AND HAPPY BEEING A VARY OPEN SATE OF THE TIPS. FOR REFERENCE WE WERE THINKING ABOUT MIMICKING A DOGS TAIL THAT STARTS TO WIGGLE WHEN THE DOG IS HAPPY BUT RETRACTS WHEN THE DOG IS SCARED/ANGRY - WE WHERE THINKING ABOUT A VERY SUBTLE ANIMATION JUST AT THE END OF HER ANTENNAS HERE

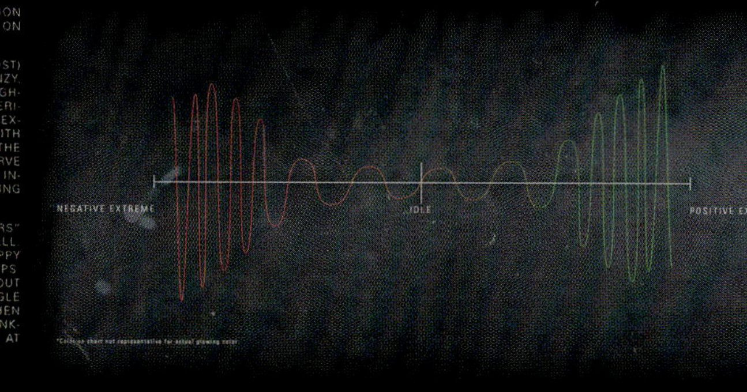

TRIXTER

"Designing characters is collaborative and goes through evolutions as each subsequent department tackles the reality of making the character real," Andy Park says. "It starts with us [Visual Development]. Then the costume designer [Judianna Makovsky] makes the costume come alive. She added elements and details to her costume that were very elegant and in keeping with the feel necessary for her story. With characters like Mantis, there is a practical-effects element due to her makeup, hair, and any other aspect needed to make her alien. At this stage, James started to feel like Mantis' facial features needed to be simplified. And once Pom Klementieff was cast, and tests were done on her face, it was clear that simpler was the way to go. The same thinking applied to her skin color. We explored the whole gamut of colors that would best suit the character, and at the end of the day it was decided that her natural skin tone—along with the simple practical effects, hair, and makeup that were applied—really was all that was necessary to make the character come alive."

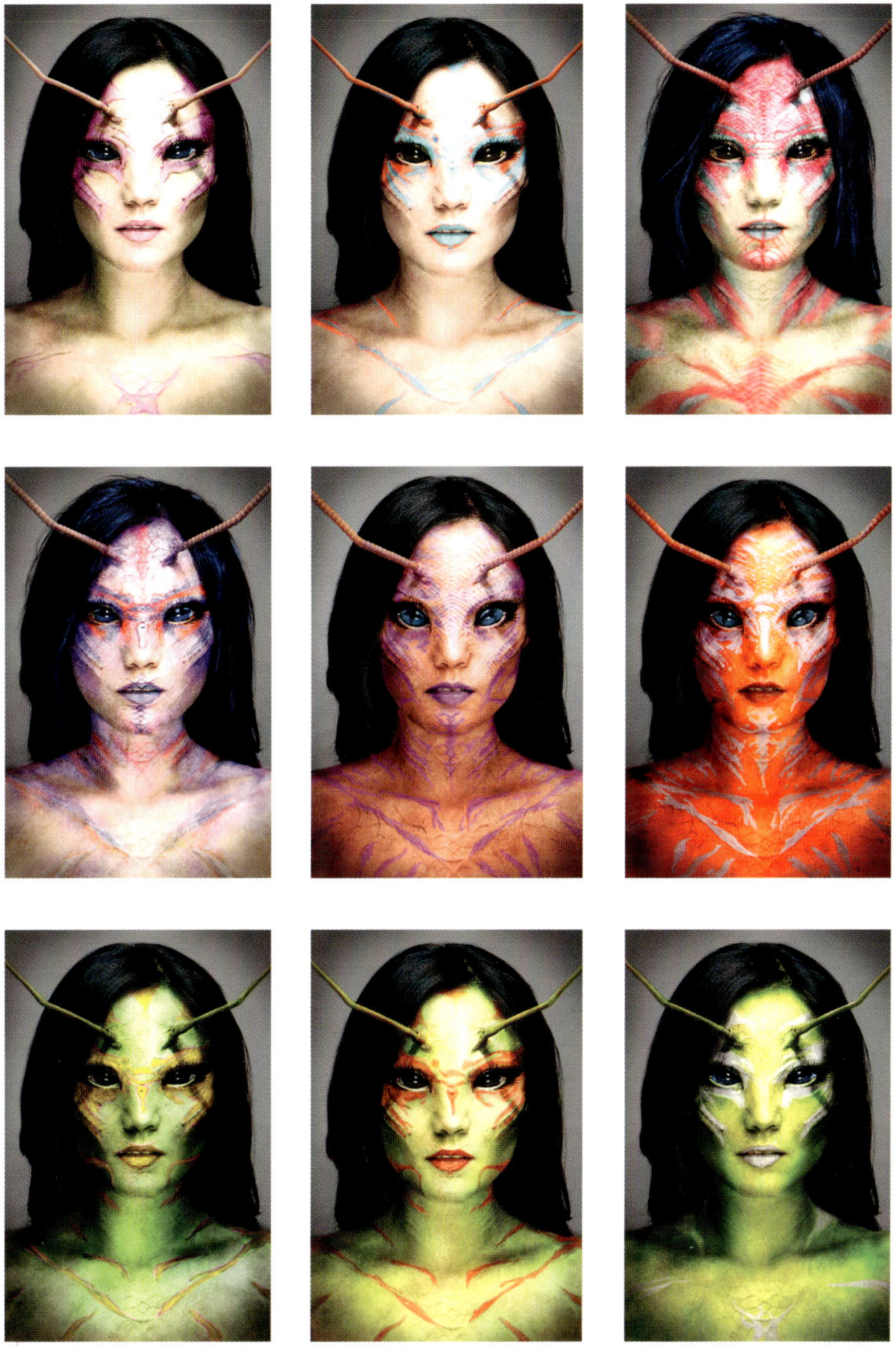

LEGACY EFFECTS and NEMOLATO

FUENTEBELLA

Early concepts took Mantis in various directions—some far more bug-like, others more abstract and alien—the key element being to connect her aesthetic to Ego's. The initial design phase allowed ample opportunity for exploration and discovery, Visual Development Illustrator Rodney Fuentebella says. "I wanted to create a Mantis that played with the idea of balancing beauty and grotesque. I wanted to convey that she is innocent, but still powerful, in my designs—always trying to make her feel different than the other species."

MARANTZ

SZE

MARANTZ

"Having Rocket stalk his unsuspecting prey from above provided an opportunity to use a dramatic angle to illustrate the moment," Visual Development Illustrator Jackson Sze says. "By creating a murky forest with undefined shapes and confusing textures, Rocket can more effectively hide from the Ravagers, as well. The idea is to showcase Rocket in complete control of the situation, as he often is."

SZE

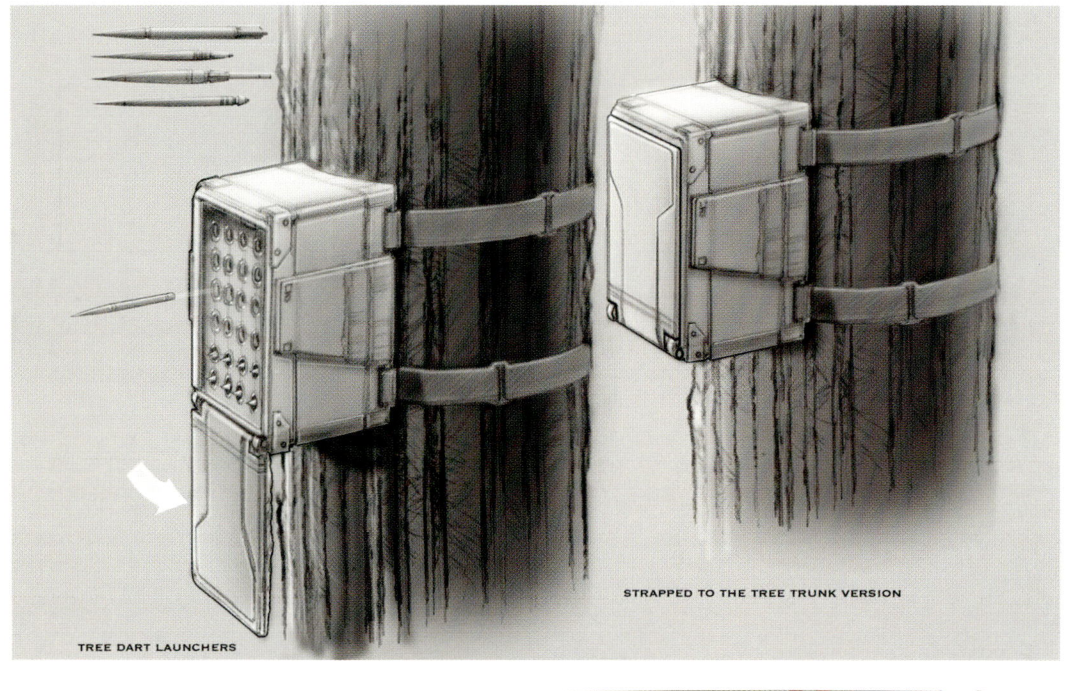

ROCKET'S ARSENAL

"Rocket has always been my favorite in the *Guardians of the Galaxy* universe, so it was a treat to draw a slew of props for this little guy," Prop Illustrator John Eaves says. "For one of the earlier scenes in the film, Rocket sets a series of traps in the forest. We first had to come up with a few ideas for boxes that would house a series of darts, mounted on the surrounding tree trunks. The concept for the boxes went through the approval process quickly, while most of the design time was on which dart concept to use. In the end, a blunt-nosed version with a rather long needle coming off of the front was chosen. Next came mines that would activate once stepped on, then have a delay until Rocket would use his detonator to set them all off. For the detonator, we drew a slew of versions based on video-game controllers with a mass of piping and wires. As in all of Rocket's devices, they had to have a signature style of elements massed together, then hastily hardwired to make all the elements work.

"The sticky discs were probably the one prop we drew more versions of than any other single piece for the film. We added a pattern across the top and an activation light in the center. To trigger the sticky discs, we also came up with a wrist remote that Rocket would use to give those who had been hit with a disc a rather severe electric sahock. As usual, a variety of ideas were drawn, and in the end we had come up with a long bracelet/gauntlet-style piece with all the electronics in an open area on the top."

TRIXTER

DIAZ

TRIXTER

EAVES

EAVES

BERHERT FOREST ATTACK STORYBOARDS | DELLINGER

previous SZE

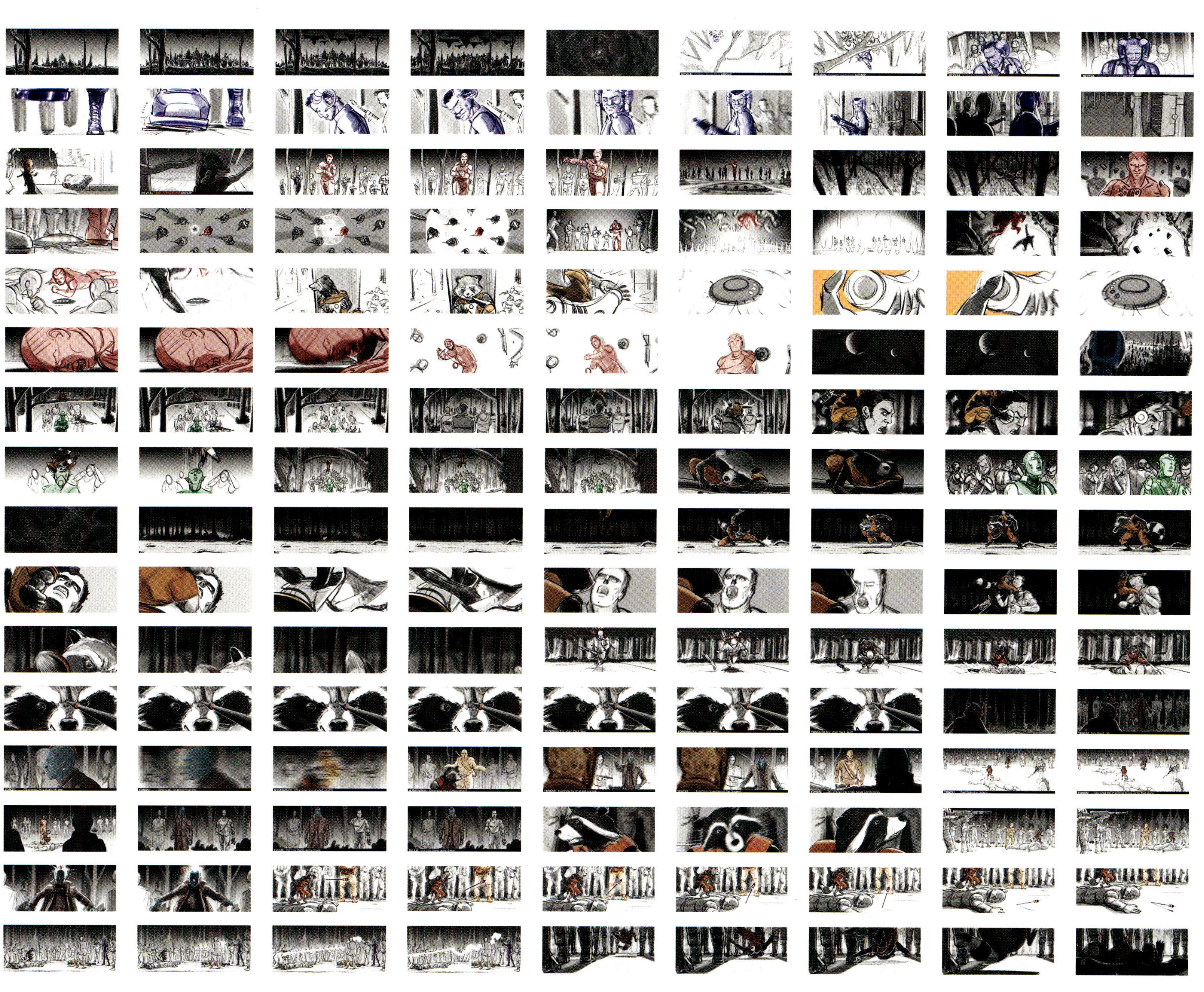

IRON LOTUS

00100010
yonou

CHAPTER 3
CONTRAXIA

WELCOME TO CONTRAXIA: a neon-laden tundra where debauchery rules, most notably at the Iron Lotus brothel. "Contraxia is the red-light district of their galaxy, populated by pirates, criminals, and other riffraff—each looking for love in robotic places," Production Designer Scott Chambliss says. "It's raw and colorful and fun, just like everything that takes place there." Chambliss says he "exploited the contrasts" between Contraxia's desolate landscape and fluorescent cityscape, all neon lights and tacky facades. "If you're going to make a playground for space pirates, who designed it? What's it made of? What are they comfortable in? The first thing that came to mind to me was a whole yard of repurposed junk—where old spaceships are cast away, where industrial materials that aren't of use anymore are just left to rot. My thought was that these guys or their friends made it themselves. Basically, somebody who was enterprising realized there was no good place to hang out anywhere. So he or she just looked at what was around and started cobbling it together. You can think of how Times Square used to be back in the '70s and '80s, or various European districts that are all about people gathering and interacting. And like Las Vegas, often there's neon—it's a lure to get people in."

previous KUTSCHE, BACH, and SCHARF

BACH and LUKOWSKI

SELLARS

BEN-MIMOUN

TRIXTER

BACH and SHERRIFF

SZE

LOVE BOTS

"From Hans Bellmer's *La poupée*—his sculptures of distorted and fetishistic dolls—to the sexy female cyborgs in Masamune Shirow's *Ghost in the Shell*, to the glossy white-robot version of Björk in Chris Cunningham's music video 'All Is Full of Love,' to the recent movie *Ex Machina*, there's always been a fascination with well-proportioned female cyborgs," Visual Development Illustrator Michael Kutsche says. "Needless to say, I was more than excited when James asked us to do our take on them for *Guardians of the Galaxy Vol. 2*. But as much as I found myself inspired by the aforementioned depictions, the challenge was to come up with something original that was clearly distinct from them. What I ended up with after quite a few iterations has that '80s retro charm, which the first movie pulled off so successfully, but combined with the timeless elegance of the *Maschinenmensch* in Fritz Lang's *Metropolis*."

KUTSCHE

METHOD STUDIOS

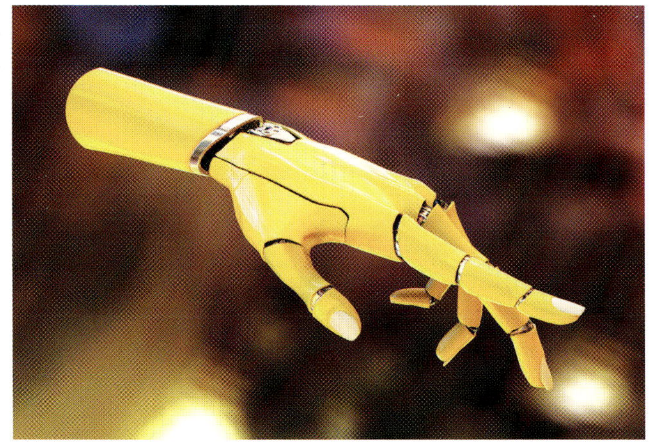

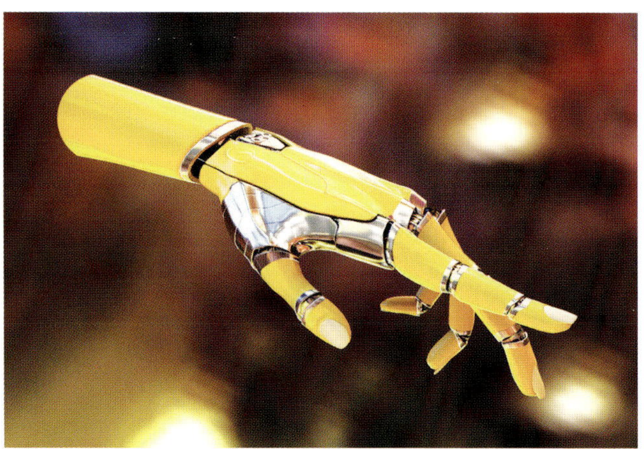

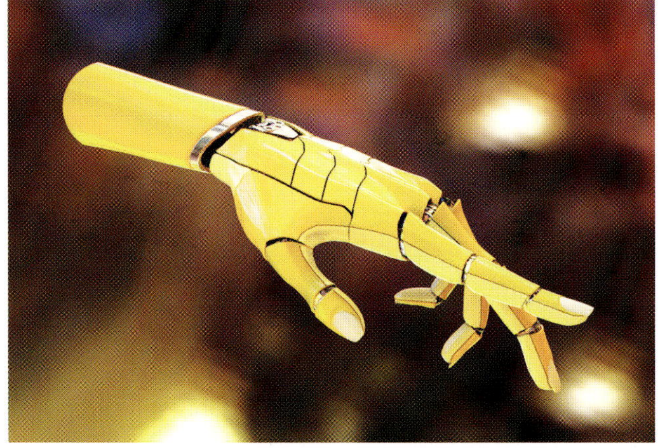

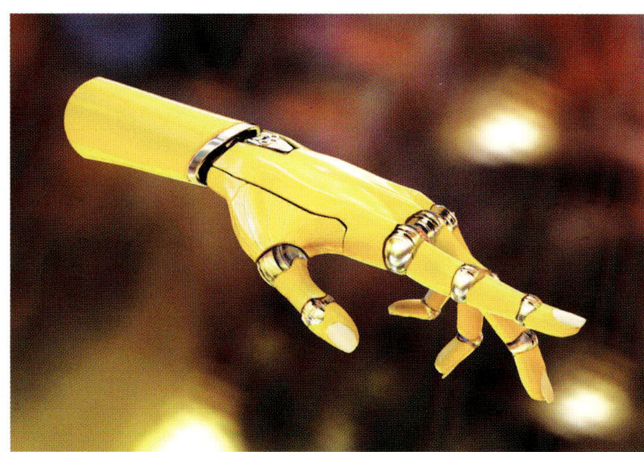

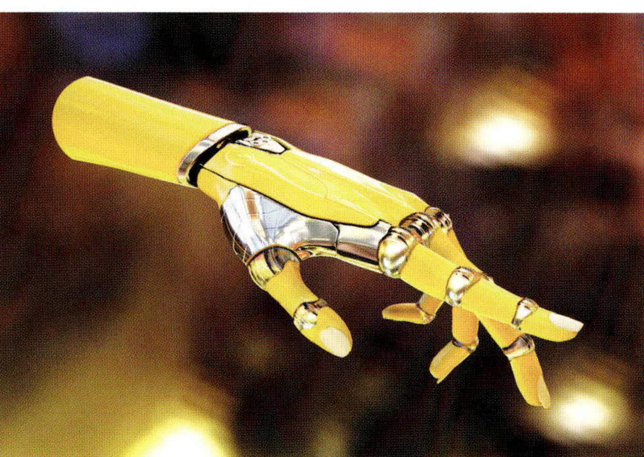

"What makes someone attractive varies widely from person to person," Visual Development Illustrator Jackson Sze says. "We created a variety of designs to cater to an array of tastes. Variety was important, as these bots were purchased by a diverse clientele. Some features were broadly generalized, while others were more specific. One design called for anime-like features with bigger-than-normal eyes. Trying to capture a wide variety of tastes that everyone was happy with proved challenging and time-consuming. There are many fantastic and memorable humanoid-robot designs in film history, from *Metropolis* to *Buck Rogers* to *Star Wars*. Everything was looked at and studied. Modern consumer appliances, with seamless constructions, and prosthetic limbs were referenced as well."

TRIXTER

SZE

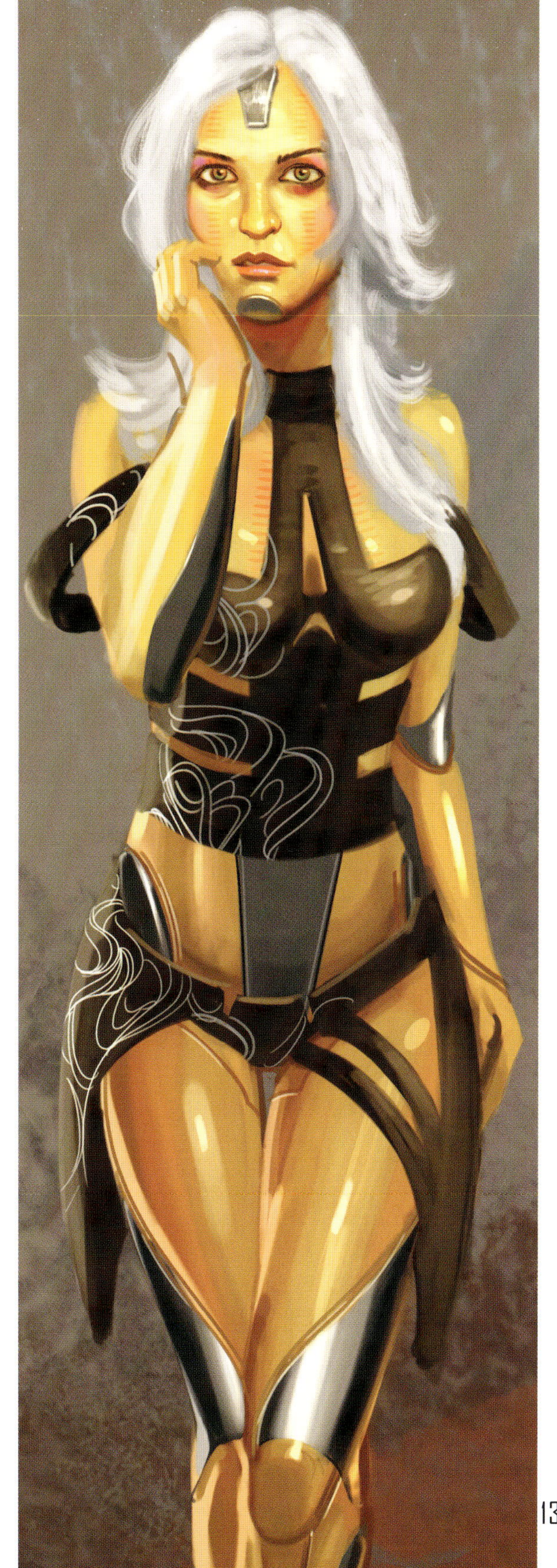

YONDU

The Ravagers' blue-skinned leader, Yondu Udonta, returns to the screen with a similar look, but a new fin. "We established Yondu's look successfully in the first film, so I didn't make many changes to his look with a new concept," Visual Development Illustrator Rodney Fuentebella says. "His aesthetic defines the Ravager look—so there also wasn't a story reason to alter his costume. I did do a lengthy exploration on the fin, though. We knew early on Yondu was going to lose his fin, so it was a design element I started on at the beginning of development. This new fin is something that really brings back the look from the comics. In the first film, I designed the fin to be more minimal and to show off the mechanical, sci-fi element of the fin. In this version, I wanted to make sure the design was different and more of a standout piece. Looking at how large and bold the fin was in the comics, I tried to adapt that into a realistic piece that felt practical—

FUENTEBELLA

FUENTEBELLA

or at least practical enough. The conceptualization process was something I deemed 'Fin 2.0'—finding the right level of refinement to generate a stronger first read, while intricately placing high-tech cut lines for close-ups. Since his overall look wasn't changing, the new fin really needed to stand out."

HARGREAVES

EAVES

THE RAVAGERS

For a ragtag band of ne'er-do-wells, the Ravagers' costumes are deceptively uniform. "The Ravagers are like an outer-space motorcycle gang; that's kind of where we started with their look," Costume Designer Judianna Makovsky says. "If you look closely, there are really only five different shapes of garment that we then tailor to each person and add different details to individualize each Ravager. In the first film, there weren't women Ravagers, so that was a challenge—how to adapt the look for women and do them in different colors. The red seemed to work really well for everything, but James mentioned he wanted some yellow Ravagers—which really worried me at first. How do you make that look good? But surprisingly, in the end, the yellow Ravagers were almost everyone's favorite. James has such a great color sense. He's very brave with color, which is nice. A lot of directors won't go there, so it's extremely liberating that I can experiment with all this color."

DIAZ

DIAZ

TASERFACE

A fearsome, mechanical maniac in the comics, Taserface was a blip in the *Guardians of the Galaxy* mythology. However, due to his unique—and, yes, ridiculous—name, he was a character James Gunn was eager to introduce among the Ravagers' ranks. "Taserface is one of Yondu's enforcers, one of many Ravagers—but he doesn't really love the way things are going," Executive Producer Louis D'Esposito says. "All these Ravagers joined up with Yondu to be bad guys, and Taserface thinks that Yondu is slipping—that he's leaning toward the side of good—so he stages a mutiny against Yondu."

"Taserface was described to me as needing to be very scary-looking, but he wants you to think he is the absolute coolest," Visual Development Illustrator Anthony Francisco says. "I translated this into conceptualizing various things he might wear or add onto his Ravager jumpsuit—things that he thinks are badass or interesting. But ultimately, he is just trying too hard. He is also the biggest Ravager, therefore I tried to put emphasis on designing the shoulder armor to help actor Chris Sullivan look even wider. Since I was not adapting this costume from his comic counterpart, I tried to get the head to echo something from the comic book. Instead of having his signature face mask, I experimented with facial hair to get some of the shapes, and redesigned the mohawk."

FRANCISCO

LEGACY EFFECTS DIAZ

FRANCISCO

FRANCISCO

FRANCISCO

SWEET

"My conceptual angle on Taserface was about trying to incorporate the source material in with what the story needed," Concept Artist Jerad Marantz says. "I had to make sure that there were enough nods to what he looked like in the comics while giving him the signature Ravagers look that had been established in the previous film. Part of invoking his comic-book look was integrating advanced technology into his costume and weaponry."

MARANTZ

MEINERDING

HOWARD THE DUCK

"A talking duck walks into a bar...." Following his surprise cameo in the first film as a prisoner in the Collector's interstellar menagerie, everyone's favorite, foul-mouthed anthropomorphic waterfowl returns in *Guardians of the Galaxy Vol. 2*. Howard the Duck, created by writer Steve Gerber and artist Val Mayerik, made his comic-book debut in 1973 in *Adventure into Fear #19*. A denizen of Duckworld, he found himself trapped on a planet dominated by "hairless apes"—Earth, to you and me—and he's been trying to make the best of a bad situation ever since. We last saw Howard sharing an alien drink with a shell-shocked Collector amid the wreckage of his museum, and we find him here having another—albeit in more comfortable climes.

LANG

LANG

LANG

MEINERDING

LANG

FUENTEBELLA

STAKAR

Stakar Ogord—or Starhawk, as he's more commonly known in the comics—is a Ravager captain and Yondu's former colleague. "Stakar banished Yondu many years ago for doing something wrong," actor Sylvester Stallone says. "There's a code to the Ravagers, and Yondu broke it. It was kind of a betrayal. So when we run into one another 20 years later on Contraxia, it leads to quite a confrontation. It's very intense. Much like Peter Quill and Yondu's, Stakar and Yondu's relationship, I'd say, is also a kind of father-and-son thing."

FUENTEBELLA

"For this design, we needed to combine the established Ravager feel with some of Stakar's iconography from the comics," Rodney Fuentebella says. "I conceptualized him to look everything from strangely alien to more human—and everything in between. The energy wings, which he has in the comics, were definitely an interesting challenge. I tried putting them on the back of his head and eventually, with Andy Park's suggestion, moved them to his shoulders." According to Fuentebella, Stallone's casting helped inform the character's design. "I originally designed some ideas of Stallone being more alien—but I knew that we needed to have Stallone's presence, his expressions and facial nuances, front and center. It made his overall design more about the costume than altering his face in any major capacity."

MARTINEX

Martinex, another Ravager and close friend of Stakar, is fully composed of organic, silicon-isotope crystal. "For Martinex, they had already done design work and VFX work, but it was not reading as strong as they would have liked," Visual Development Illustrator Ian Joyner says. "The thought was to take the crystal, human shape, and add cracks and overlap to show that the movement could naturally happen without warping too much. Looking at natural elements for the crystal and rougher areas, we tried to find a way to draw focus to the features without letting the refraction/reflection overwhelm the performance."

"To conceptualize the look for his costume, I first looked at his relationship with Stakar and the other Ravagers," Rodney Fuentebella says. "Stakar is wearing a deep blue, so I started with putting Martinex in blue, too. From there, it was all about establishing history and personality."

FUENTEBELLA

TRIXTER

TRIXTER

SUMMERS

CHARLIE-27

In the comics, Charlie-27 has been biogenetically engineered to withstand Jupiter's gravity, which is triple that of Earth—resulting in a hulking body, and the strength and endurance to match. "I referenced the iconic look of Charlie-27 straight from the comic pages," Jackson Sze says. "The bold red cross of his bandoliers and strong yellow color was given a Ravager spin as far as the details of the costume go."

"I liked the idea of Charlie-27 being really wide, really broad," Anthony Francisco says. "That was a trademark of his in the comic book. It gives him a great visual dynamic when standing next to Stakar, Martinex, and Aleta. Like Jackson, I also wanted to adapt the signature elements of his costume from the comics into the aesthetic of the film franchise. That meant finding a way to integrate the square buckles and patchwork on his jumpsuit—also keeping the strong yellow color."

FRANCISCO

SZE

ALETA

Aleta Ogord was Stakar's wife in the comics, capable of transforming light into a solid state to create weapons and shields. In the film, little is revealed about her history, outside of her involvement with Stakar's group of Ravagers. "Aleta's costume was referenced from the comic pages, as well," Jackson Sze says. "That's where we usually start a design on an established comic character. The fact that she was a Ravager helped us focus the look and functionality of the design. The chest armor she wears in the comics was given a more piecemeal, weathered treatment to give her a little history. I also did a number of passes on hairstyles to accentuate her character. James was specific with instructions in the later design rounds. He wanted long hair that covered her face, helping lend personality to this character."

SZE

MAINFRAME

"Part of the fun of the *Guardians of the Galaxy* world is the opportunity to introduce new alien characters, and that these characters can be creatures or anything nonhuman in look," Visual Development Supervisor Andy Park says. "Mainframe was described to me by James as being just a box or a head of some sort. This in turn could be plugged into different objects that she could control."

Visual Development Illustrator Tully Summers worked with Park to conceptualize the design. "The design brief for Mainframe was to come up with a *Flash Gordon*/pulp-style robot head that sits independently on a table, and has the ability to plug into and control different bodies and vehicles," Summers says. "The challenge was to design something that could emote and portray character without the use of a body to aid in emotive gestures. I settled on a swiveling neck base that would still let Mainframe turn her head to focus on people around the table, a mouth-grill light set, and eye shutters that would change shape to portray different expressions. Junior Illustrator Melissa Encinas did a brilliant animation test that proved it could successfully emote. James requested Mainframe's head be housed in a cage-like cube that could be picked up and plugged into her various bodies."

SUMMERS

SUMMERS

SZE

FRANCISCO

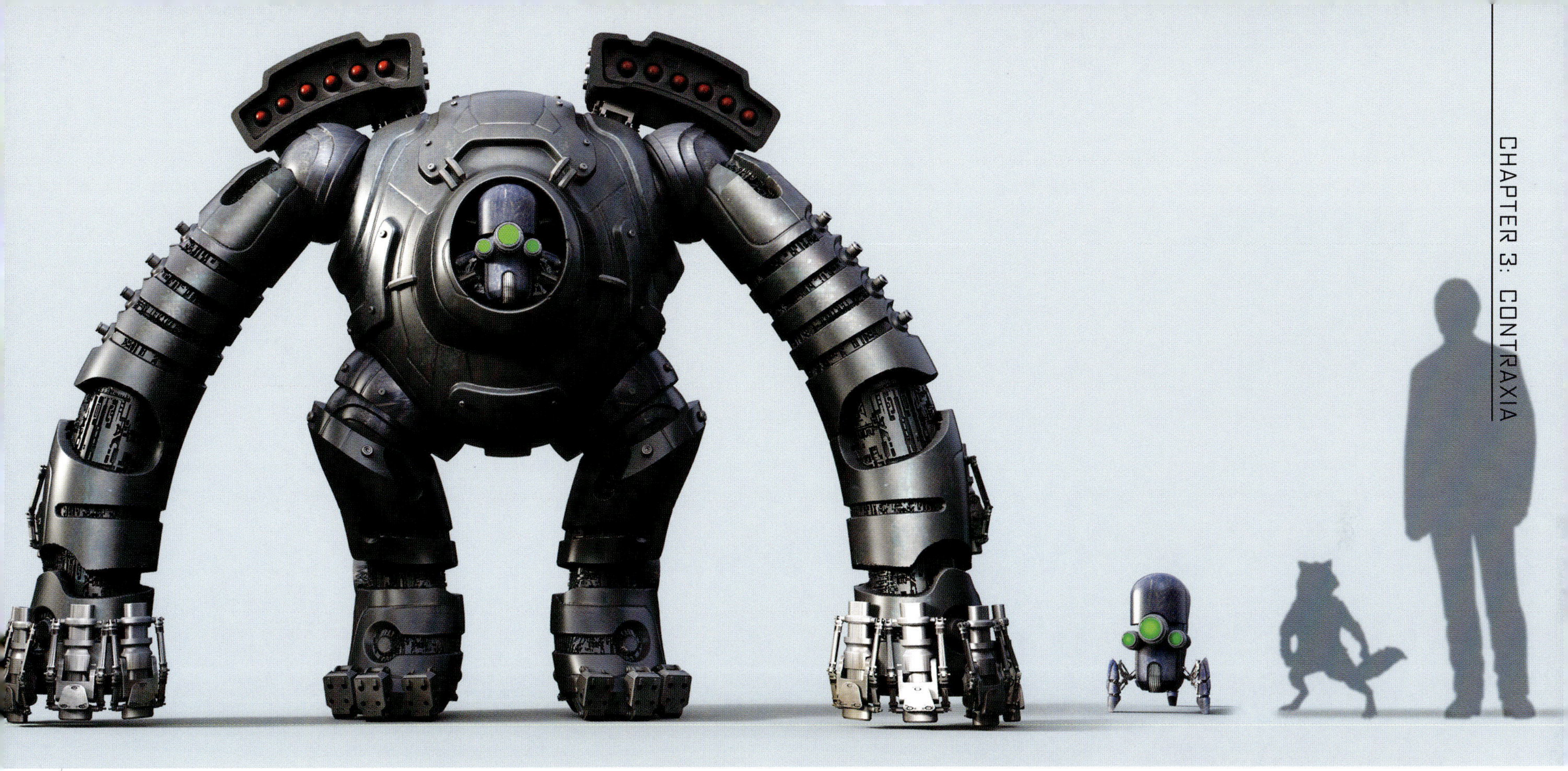

SUMMERS

"Given limited comic-book references, we had a good deal of freedom in coming up with the look of this robot," Jackson Sze says. "We knew James liked the *Metropolis*, early sci-fi aesthetics, so I worked toward those visuals. Early on, we tried to do as many variations as possible to gauge what James had in mind for this character. I believe it only took a couple rounds of feedback for Tully Summers to get what James wanted."

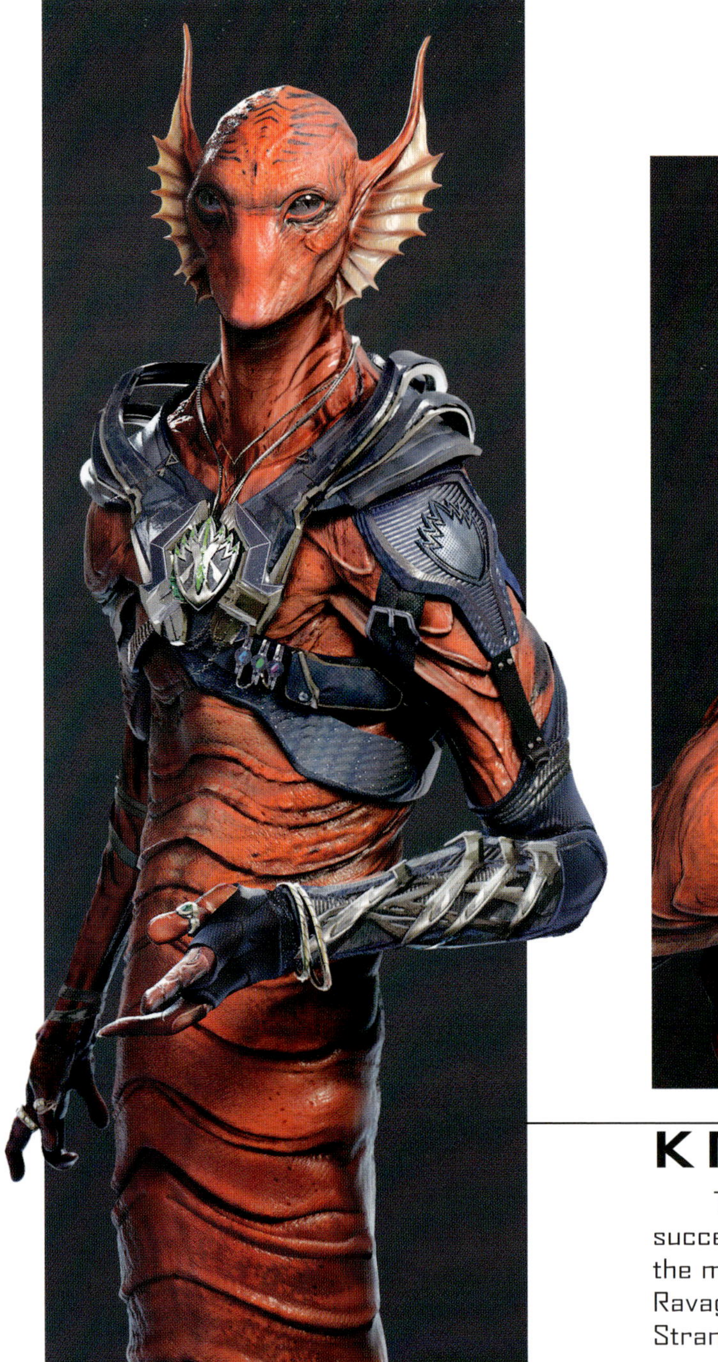

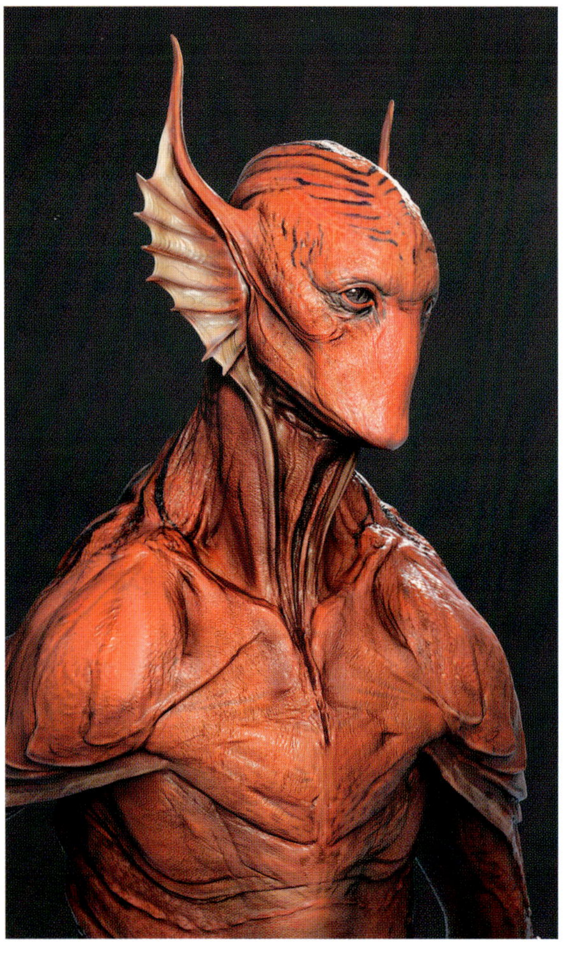

KRUGARR

The comic-book Krugarr—one of a race of long-lived, wormlike creatures called the Lem—succeeds Doctor Strange as Sorcerer Supreme in the 22nd century, with Strange taking on the mantle of his own mentor, the Ancient One. In the film, Krugarr is a member of Stakar's Ravagers. "Krugarr was a fun one to try and visualize," Ian Joyner says. "A cosmic, Doctor Strange-type character, mouthless, with the body of a worm. The initial instinct was to go full-on creepy with his look, but we also wanted him to have a soul and personality, which was a fun balance to try and reach. One of the interesting aspects of his design was figuring out a costume that felt both sci-fi and mystic, all while keeping him in line with the Ravagers' look."

JOYNER

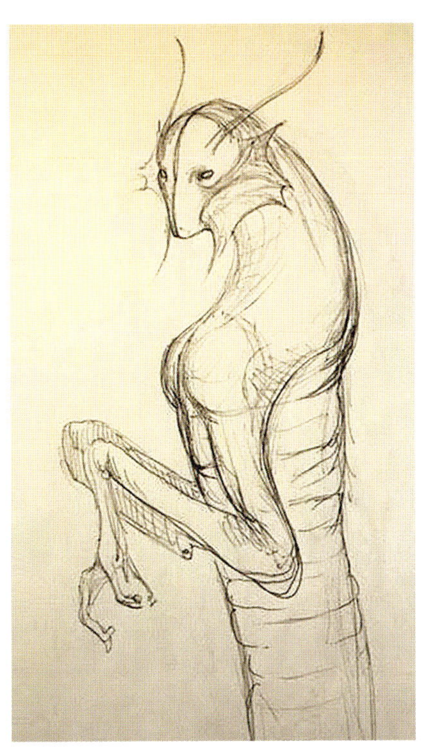

SEKERIS

SZE

JOYNER

JOYNER and TRIXTER

“James wanted to stick to the character’s comic reference with regards to his look,” Jackson Sze says. “There is an emphasis on Krugarr’s hands and fingers, as he communicates using hand gestures and glyphs drawn in the air. Since there’s an aspect of mysticism to the character, ornaments and accessories were explored as well.”

SUMMERS

THE ECLECTOR

Yondu's ship, the *Eclector*, helped save the day at the end of the first film by delivering Ravager reinforcements to Xandar during Ronan's attack. Industrially strong and dynamically eclectic in its design, the vessel mirrors its crew. Scott Chambliss was eager to explore additional detailing to add even more character to the ship. "The wonderful *Eclector* design from the first film didn't need fussing with—but because I'm a designer, I can't help myself. What I chose to do was to create a vocabulary of negative spaces within the previously overall solid mass of the ship. The point was to give the ship a more detailed, sculptural quality, one that would support the visual concept of the great big hulk's ability to separate into smaller ships—or Quadrants—that could function independently of each other."

The ship's interior features sleeping quarters, control rooms, and prison cells—and, of course, a bar. Chambliss embraced the Ravagers' collective personality to determine the tone and atmosphere. "The Ravagers are intergalactic, rust-bucket pirates picking up whatever they want, wherever they want. They're attracted to shiny things, and they don't bathe. All that adds up to the *Eclector's* color and texture palette."

THOMPSON

THOMPSON

ECLECTOR DOCKING BAY

SHERRIFF

MILANO

BACH

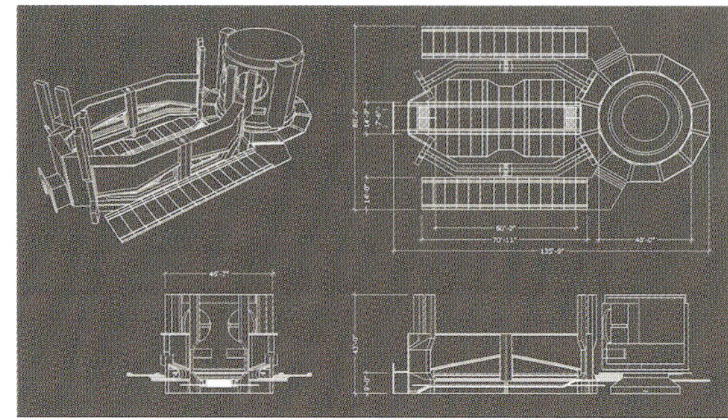

***ECLECTOR* CENTRAL ROOM** KADONAGA

BACH

previous SHERRIFF

KADONAGA

BACH

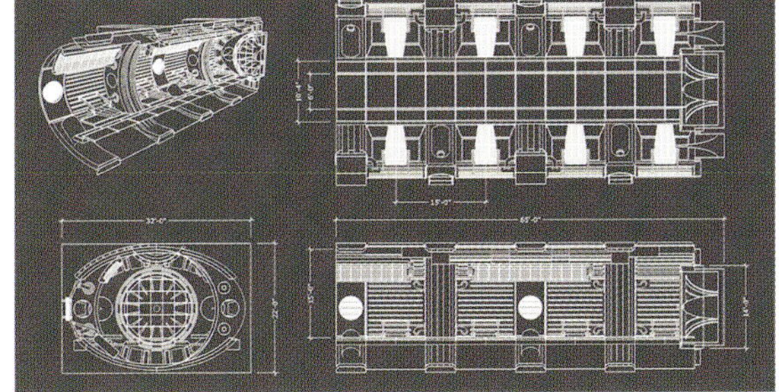

MARTINEZ

ECLECTOR CELL BLOCK

During Taserface's mutiny, Yondu is thrown in his own ship's prison. "The cellblock was first seen in the previous film," Chambliss says. "Yondu's cell is a disused industrial alcove in the mechanical section of the ship that has been ad hoc repurposed into a holding cell. Eclectic assemblage and usage is the very foundation of the *Eclector* ship's design in both films." The stark differences between the *Eclector* and the film's more organic environments provided a welcome challenge, Chambliss says. "It was a fantastic contrast to the process of designing all things related to Ego!"

SHERRIFF

"This keyframe mirrors the slow-walk-toward-camera moment the Guardians of the Galaxy had in the first film," Andy Park says. "But this time it's Yondu, Rocket, and little Groot. It's the oddest little trio, but it's a powerful shift in the dynamics of their relationships—a real turning point in the film. I had nothing but fun painting this pivotal—and hilarious—moment."

PARK

***ECLECTOR* SECURITY ROOM**

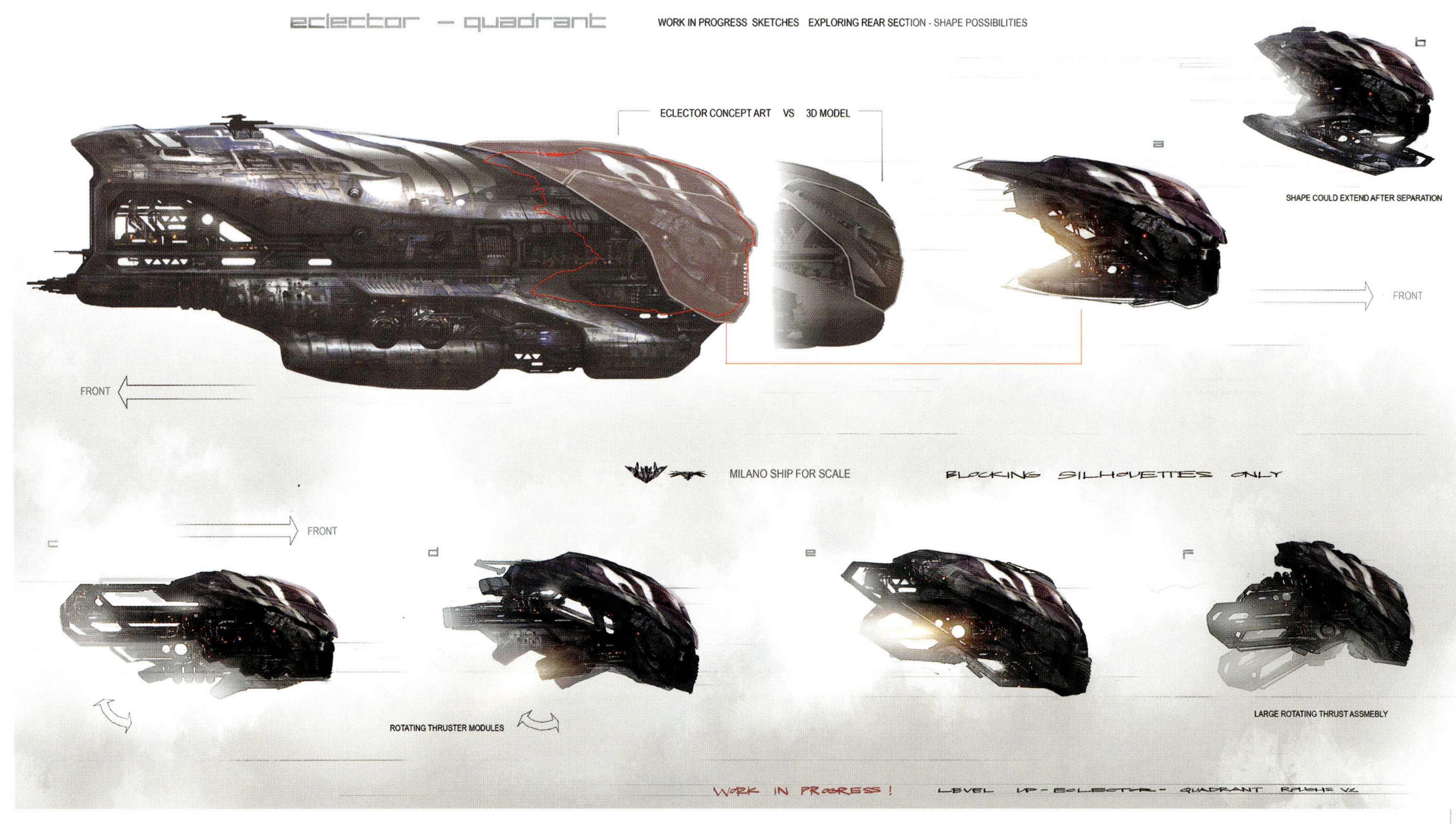

THE QUADRANT

Every scoundrel needs a contingency plan for those inevitable tight spots, and Yondu is no exception. "The Quadrant is the *Air Force One* section of the *Eclector*, able to detach and function as a faster and more agile fighter ship," Scott Chambliss says. "Yondu's captain's quarters are located there, as is the first-class cabin's bar—a scene that was ultimately cut from the script, unfortunately. A Ravagers first-class bar doesn't look much like anyone else's idea of such a thing."

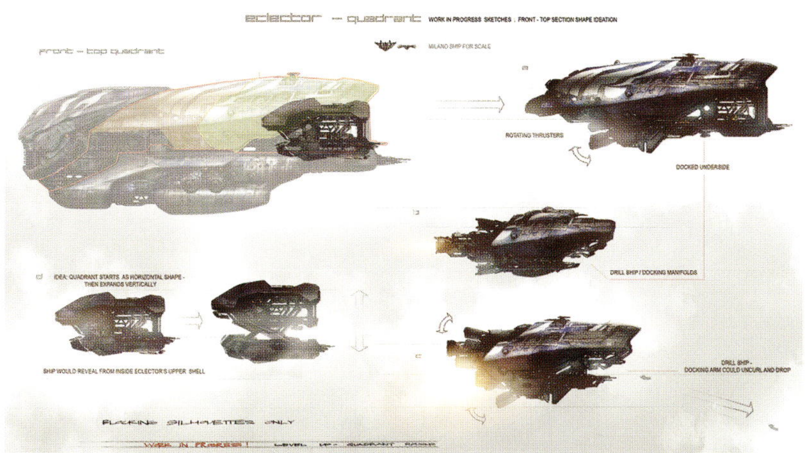
eclector – quadrant WORK IN PROGRESS SKETCHES : FRONT - TOP SECTION SHAPE IDEATION
MILANO SHIP FOR SCALE
front – top quadrant
ROTATING THRUSTERS
DOCKED UNDERSIDE
DRILL SHIP / DOCKING MANIFOLDS
IDEA: QUADRANT STARTS AS HORIZONTAL SHAPE - THEN EXPANDS VERTICALLY
SHIP WOULD REVEAL FROM INSIDE ECLECTOR'S UPPER SHELL
DRILL SHIP - DOCKING ARM COULD UNCURL AND DROP
BLOCKING SILHOUETTES ONLY
WORK IN PROGRESS!

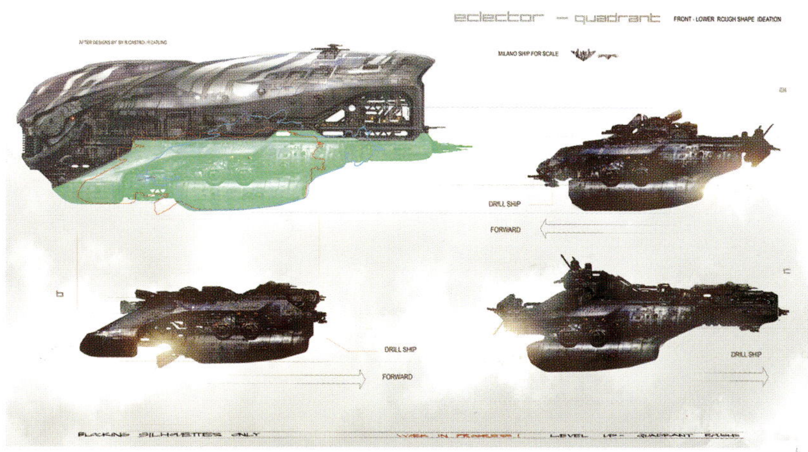
eclector – quadrant FRONT - LOWER ROUGH SHAPE IDEATION
MILANO SHIP FOR SCALE
DRILL SHIP
FORWARD
DRILL SHIP
FORWARD
DRILL SHIP
BLOCKING SILHOUETTES ONLY

QUADRANT FLIGHT DECK

HULL

HULL

HULL

QUADRANT LOADING DOCK

WEST

SHERRIFF

previous SZE

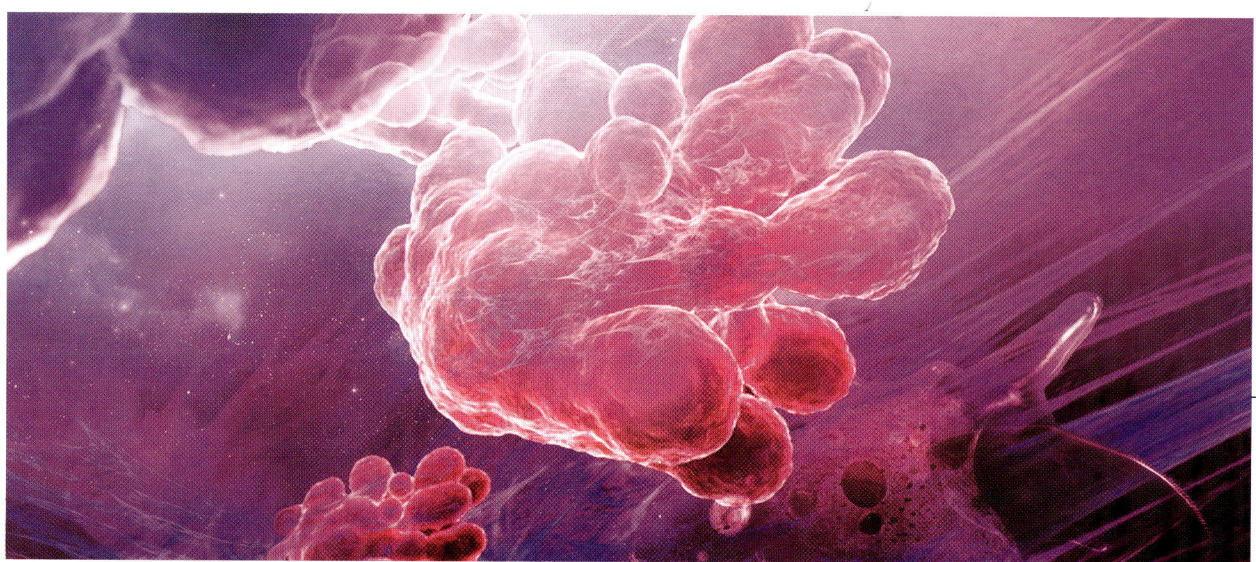

JUMP SPACE

Point-to-point portals used to traverse space by those with the navigational skill and proper technology, these gates were placed eons ago by galactic travelers. "The idea was initially conceptualized in the script, but VFX visually created the design," Visual Effects Supervisor Christopher Townsend says. "We wanted to build something that had a flashy, almost holographic look, but still felt like it existed—even if for just a brief moment—in the real world. We wanted something violent, elegant, and transient, while giving us a glimpse into the worlds beyond the gates."

SELLARS

SELLARS

SELLARS

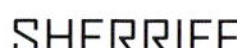

SHERRIFF

TRIXSTER

TRIXTER

CHAPTER 4
EGO

WELCOME TO EGO: the living planet—a colorful, expansive environment where nothing is what it seems. "We started with one fundamental conception: that Ego and his planet were an ultimate manifestation of self-created nature," Production Designer Scott Chambliss says. "After less-than-exciting development in that direction—it all seemed too familiar—James jettisoned that approach. He then redefined Ego as a manifestation of divine light, which freed us from the constraints of visualizing nature in a familiar way and plunged us deep into a world of creative visual abstraction to define the man and the planet. Coming up with something that has uniquely impressive qualities is always the most challenging task in designing science-fiction worlds, as it seems virtually everything has been done before. Determining a storytelling logic that an audience can grasp when faced with visual abstraction is the accompanying challenge in this task.

"The imagery must speak for itself, but keep this in mind: The design of Ego is intended to be experienced by the viewer in an entirely subjective manner. Any associative meaning a viewer may come up with comes purely from his or her own perspective. That is one of the appeals of designing abstraction worlds."

MICHLAP

MICHLAP

METHOD STUDIOS

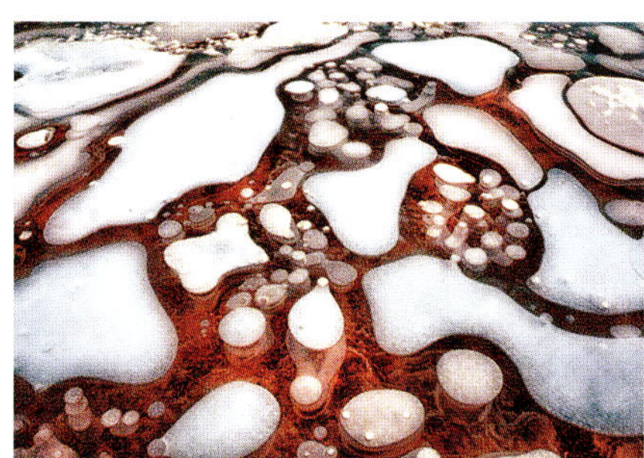

METHOD STUDIOS

METHOD STUDIOS

METHOD STUDIOS

"Knowing that we wanted to create Ego as a designed and manufactured planet while keeping it organic at the same time, we based our digital creation on Mandelbulb and Mandelbrot formulae, using algorithms to procedurally create recursive patterns," Visual Effects Supervisor Christopher Townsend says. "These elements were then converted into editable formats later so that we could assemble the interior and exterior as completely virtual CG jigsaw puzzles of different pieces. These fully CG environments were then combined with digital matte paintings on a shot-by-shot basis."

BACH

MICHLAP

BACH

BACH

previous MICHLAP

BACH

EGO'S CASTLE

Situated atop a towering mound is Ego's stronghold: a unique manifestation of the character's grandiose personality. "We used the same basic procedural fractals for the palace as for Ego's world, using Mandelbrot algorithms as the starting point," Christopher Townsend says. "We wanted an intricate, organic, almost baroque palace—but one that still echoed the visual themes we see outside, while being architecturally strong and sweeping. Contrasting with strange, chintzy murals—based on classical Roman and Greek statues crossed with Hummel sculptures and Jeff Koons art—they act as a juxtaposition to the grace of the space, while helping to tell an expositional story."

BACH and MICHLAP

"One of the circular sections and part of one of the towers were built, but the rest was virtual; for one section, we moved the whole scene outside, replacing everything except the actors," Townsend says.

previous BACH MARTINEZ

MICHLAP

MICHLAP

MICHLAP

FRANCISCO

MICHLAP

EGO'S CASTLE GARDEN

MICHLAP

EGO'S CASTLE INTERIOR

The intricate interior of Ego's palace is a sight to behold—imposing in scale, while simultaneously providing a unified sense of beauty and elegance. "It is utter fantasy without a touch of whimsicality—Ego is decidedly not a whimsical character," Scott Chambliss says. "I wanted to create something that referenced grand European baroque architecture without being so itself. The obsessive detailing is a visual reference to Ego's own megalomania. His world is intricately and complexly layered, just as he is himself."

"Using the vast array of reference that Scott [Chambliss] and his team created, and combined with James's clear direction in terms of general forms and color palettes, we did some early spatial tests in previsualization from those, we determined what should be built as a practical set," Christopher Townsend says. "It became apparent that in order to have a vast, interactively lit volume, with continual growth or destruction going on, we needed to heavily rely on VFX to create the environments. Practical sculpted ground planes were created, hewn from solid chunks of polystyrene, then painted and dressed to look like the cavern floors, upon which the actors stood. Ultimately, some of this was used in camera, but generally the environments were virtual. We constantly referred back to the artwork as a guide to the final look."

SELLARS

NOWAK

SELLARS

EGO'S SLEEPING QUARTERS

"These are guest pavillions; in theory, each of the Guardians had one of their own," Chambliss says. "I designed them to be arrayed along a hillside, much like the homes terracing the mountainside in Positano, Italy. It was a set specifically inspired by a set of Mandelbulb patterns engineered by artist Hal Tenny.

"The patterning itself is the dominant design element in the set; furnishings had to take a supporting role."

SELLARS and NOWAK

SELLARS

DOPASO

EGO'S THRONE ROOM

"Ego's grand space is more of a museum of himself and his life, and not really a throne room at all," Chambliss says. "In the original script, this space featured huge animated murals depicting different moments in his life—something he created to help the Guardians understand who, or rather what, he really is. The design sensibility for everything related to Ego is insanely detailed and mathematically complex. The one exception to this rule is Ego's own spaceship, which is deceptively simple in appearance. It is a calculated move on his part, as he maintains an air of mystery about himself at this point in the story."

FUENTEBELLA

previous FUENTEBELLA (220-221) and FRANCISCO (222-223)

In defining Ego's power set, the efforts of both the Visual Development and Visual Effects departments were necessary to craft a cohesive aesthetic that brought the script to life. "Ego is the power of the planet, and the power of the planet is Ego: That cyclic energy was developed more as the film went on, with us continually trying to find places where we could connect the two aspects," Christopher Townsend says. "Ego as a person is an extension of Ego as a planet, and we've used

subtly shared aspects in both. From the simplicity of using the signature bright-white light source, to an organic-regrowth language, through to literally having his personification in the rock formations, we've tied the two together wherever possible."

"It was a difficult task to balance something that looked humanoid but still felt uniquely alien and weird—different from what has been done already," Visual Development Illustrator Anthony Francisco says. "I looked to the ocean, and studied coral and plant life, while looking at the human nervous system to apply the specific patterns in my image."

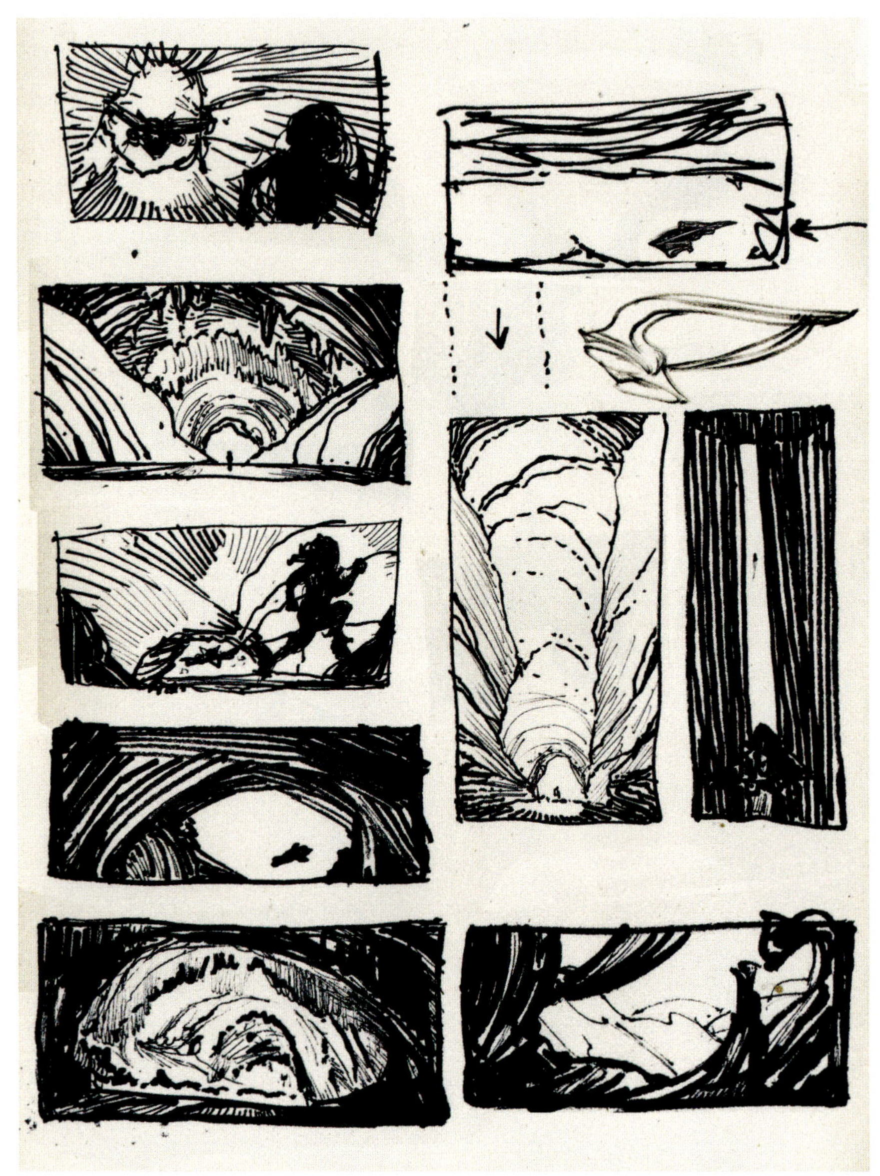

DICKENSON

NEBULA'S ATTACK

"James wanted to directly reference Hitchcock's famous *North by Northwest* sequence in which a small airplane chases Cary Grant across an open field," Scott Chambliss says. "We built an artificial red landscape for Gamora to run on while—courtesy of the magic of digital wizardry—Nebula stalks her in her spaceship."

DICKENSON

SZE

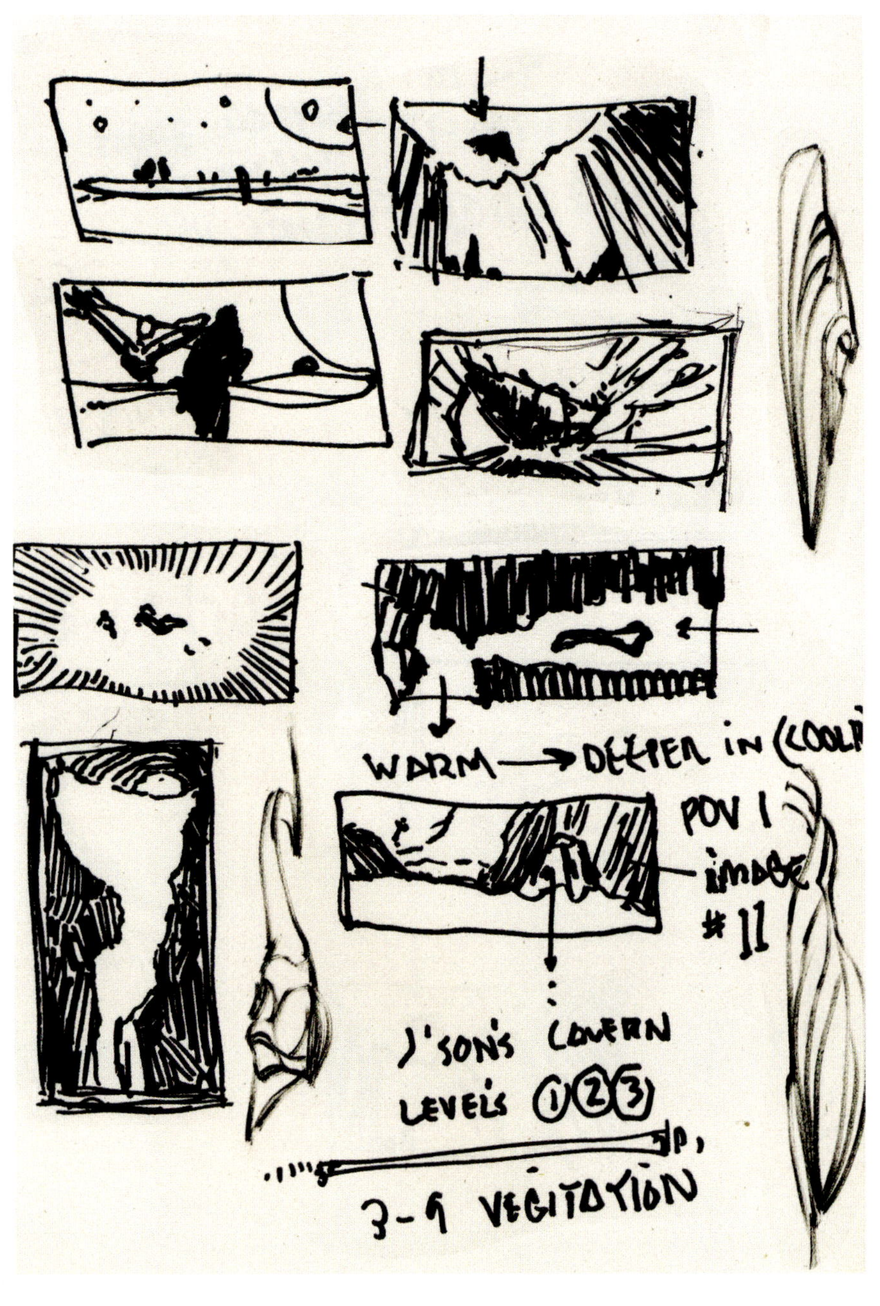

WARM → DEEPER IN (COOL
POV 1
image
#11
J'SON'S CAVERN
LEVELS 1 2 3
3-9 VEGITATION

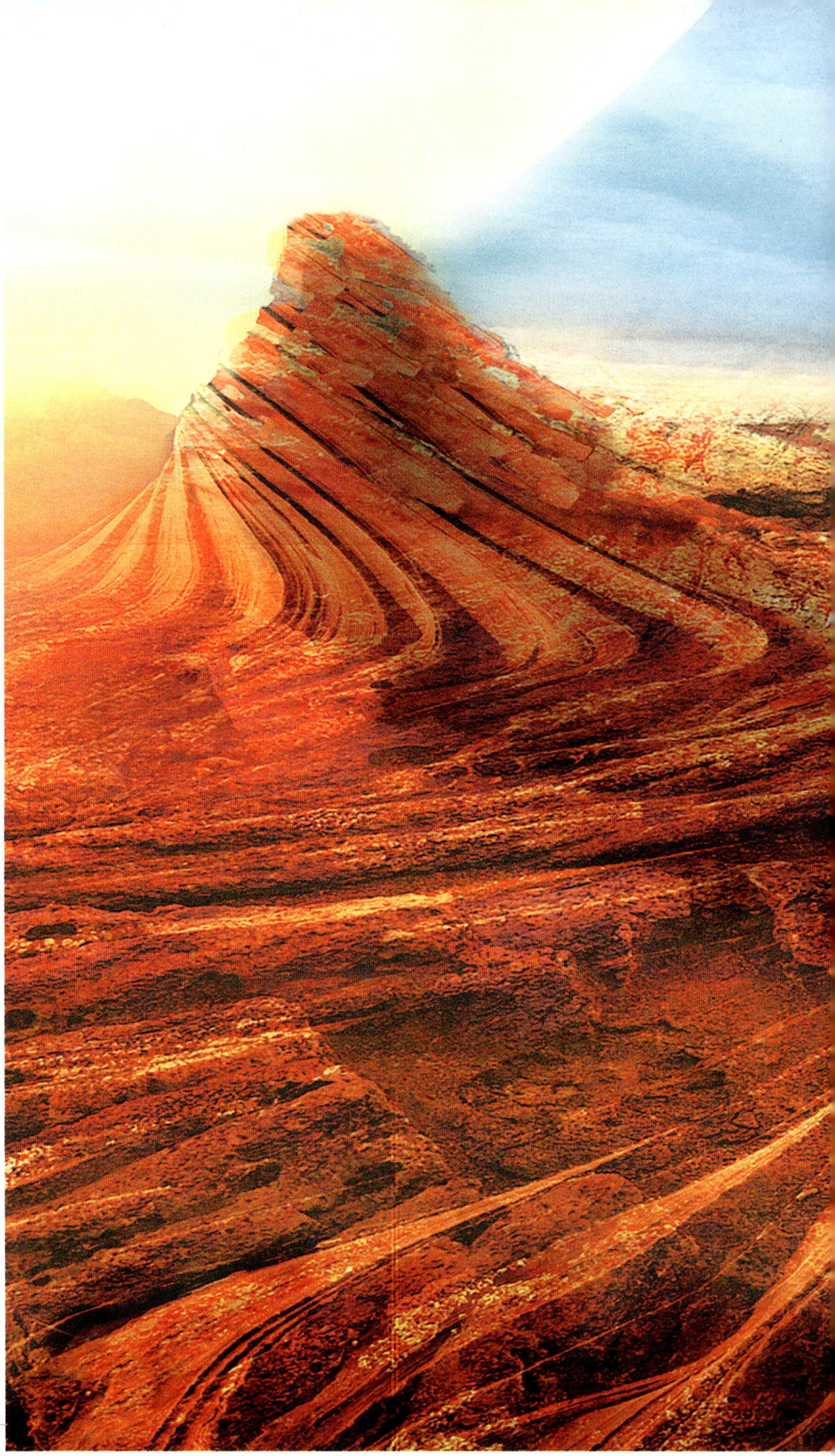

DICKENSON

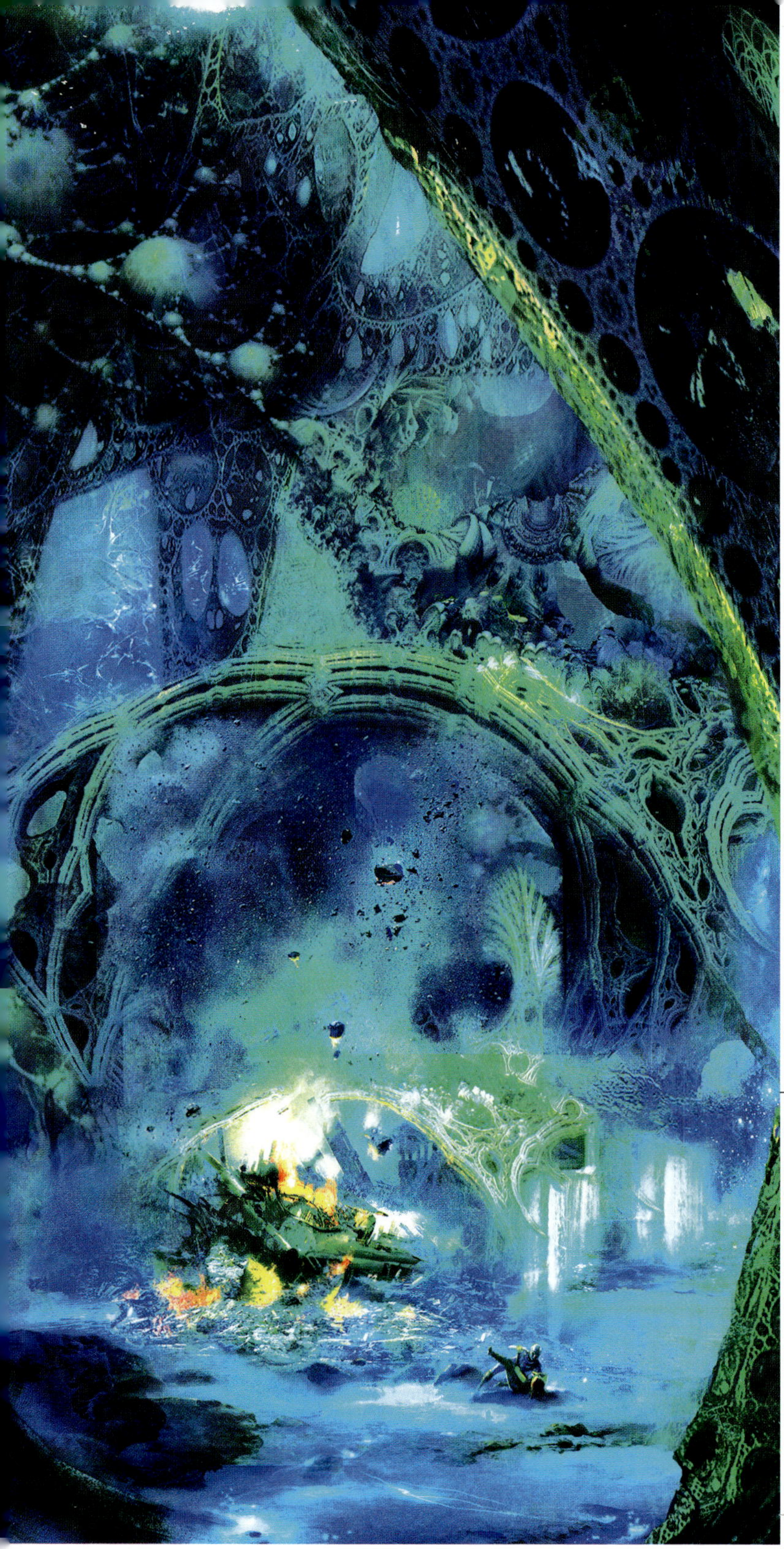

THE BONEYARD

In the wake of the *North by Northwest*-inspired sequence, Gamora and Nebula have called a truce and begun exploring the mysterious caverns deep in the planet's bowels, eventually coming upon an immensely troubling hill of bones. "In this sequence, we start on the planet's surface and wind up going deeper and deeper into the planet's core," Scott Chambliss says. "The color story begins with blue sky, golden cave walls, and red earth. The colors become deeper and darker as we progress, ultimately ending with an almost black-and-white environment for the final cavern—which you see in the center-bottom illustration above. Everything about Ego is insanely huge, including his narcissism. What better way to illustrate that than to design his self-created world as ludicrously overcomplicated. It remains for the viewer to decide if in the end the aesthetic of Ego is beautiful or monstrous—or monstrously beautiful."

previous DICKENSON

DICKENSON

MICHLAP

MICHLAP

DICKENSON

DICKENSON

MICHLAP

DICKENSON

LASER DRILL

HULL and HIURA

Yondu, Rocket, and Quill use these small vessels—docked on the Quadrant—to penetrate Ego's core. Their form language mirrors the industrial feel of both the Quadrant and the Eclector, Scott Chambliss says. "These drills are extensions of the Ravager world. I didn't want to veer too far from that aesthetic. Their design was also influenced by functionality, establishing that they could complete the action detailed in the script."

SELLARS

SHERRIFF

HULL

HULL

HULL and HIURA

PRIMARY THRUSTER ON BALL JOINT FOR AFT MANOUVERING
LASERS MODULES ON TRACKS TO ALLOW 360 DEGREE INDEPENDENT FIRING OR CONSOLIDATED FOCUSING

MICHLAP

DICKENSON

previous MICHLAP

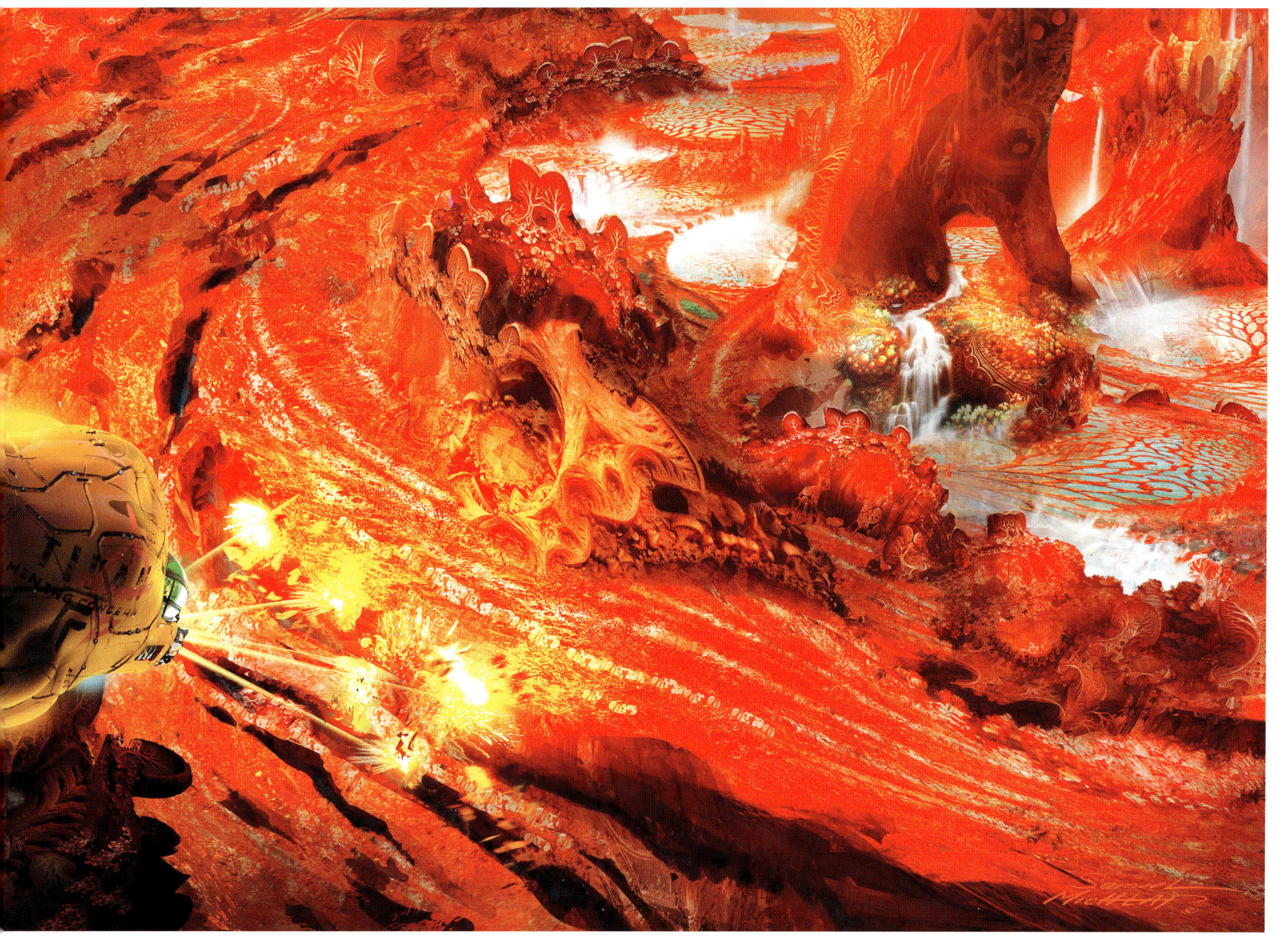

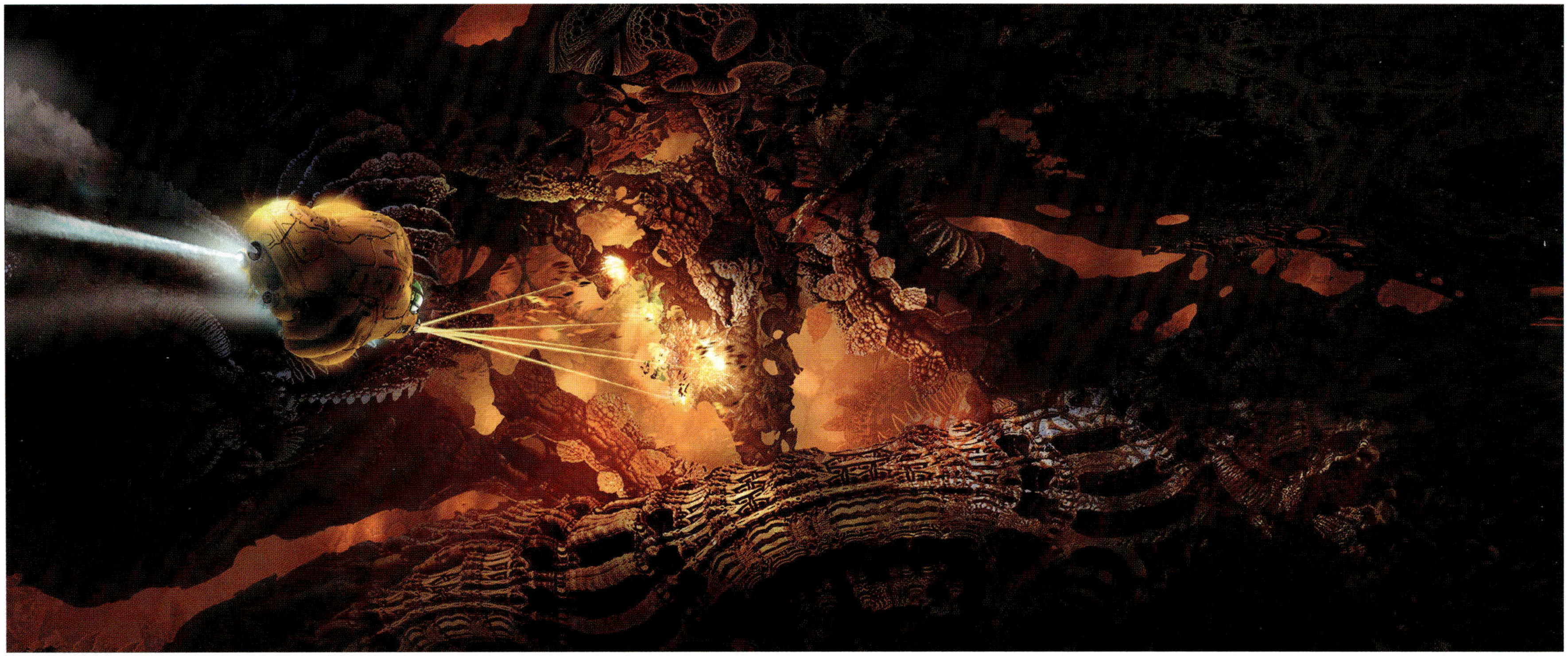

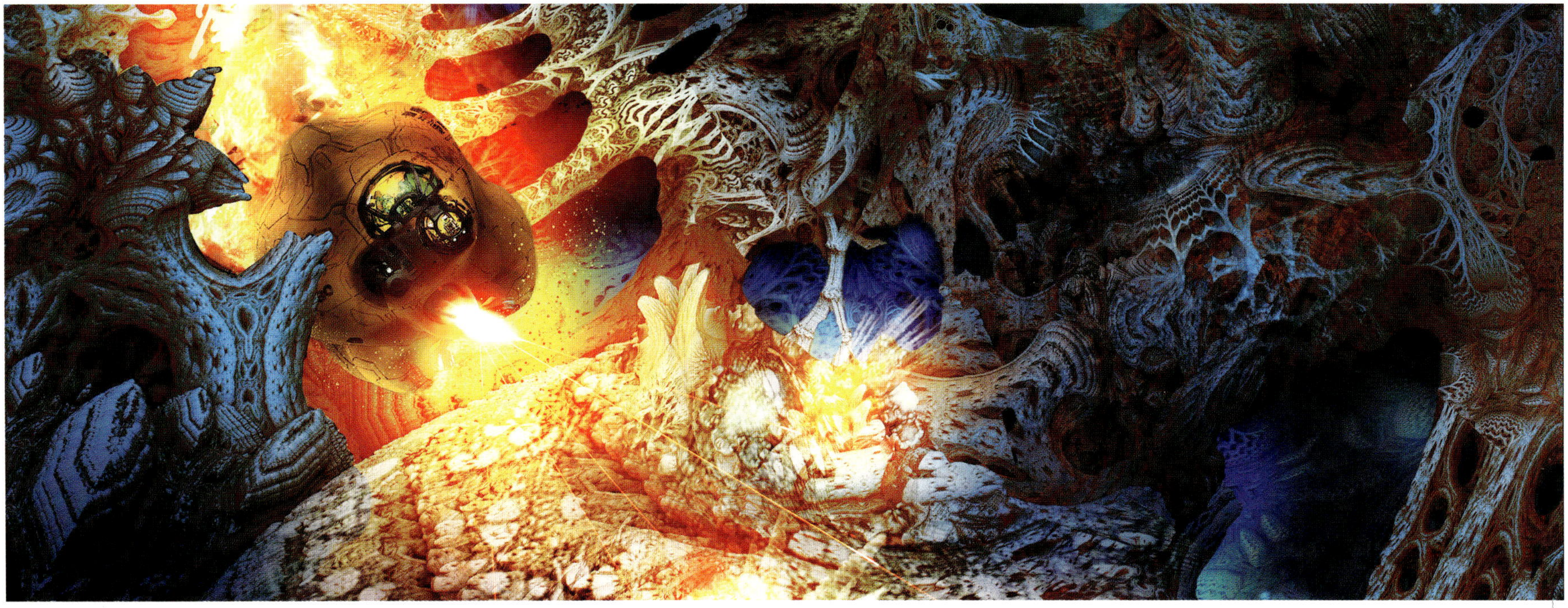

DICKENSON

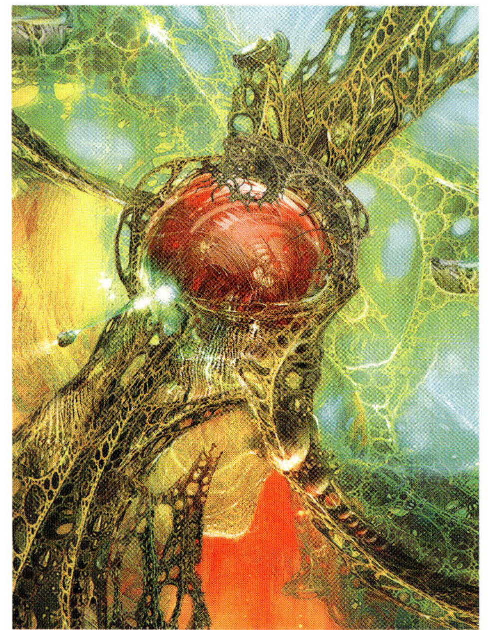

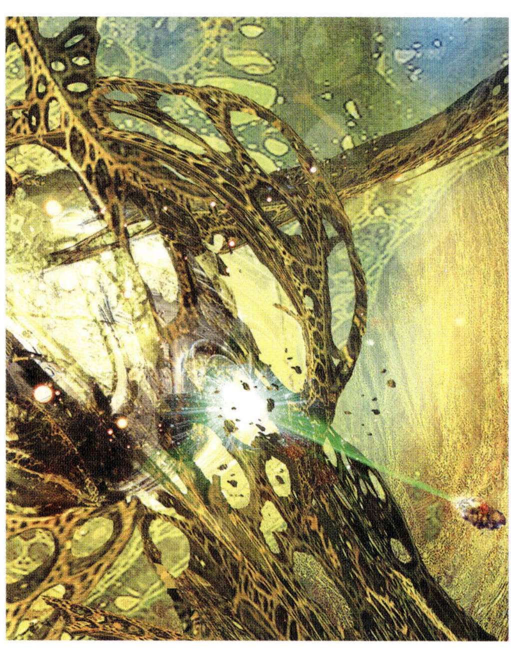

EGO'S SOUL CHAMBER

A placenta-like bubble housing Ego's brain, the Soul Chamber is in turn protected by the outer Self Chamber. "The final battle happens within the caverns of Ego's planet—a strange, massive, intricately colorful, richly saturated world; a cross between 1970s album art, an undersea reef, soaring rock towers, and huge open spaces; an organic mishmash of familiar shapes and mathematical forms," Christopher Townsend says. "The Soul Chamber is pulsating and alive, and is the relatively fragile layer upon which Groot places the bomb. The Self Chamber is the hard, rocky place through which a maze of tunnels spreads, and through which Groot takes the bomb."

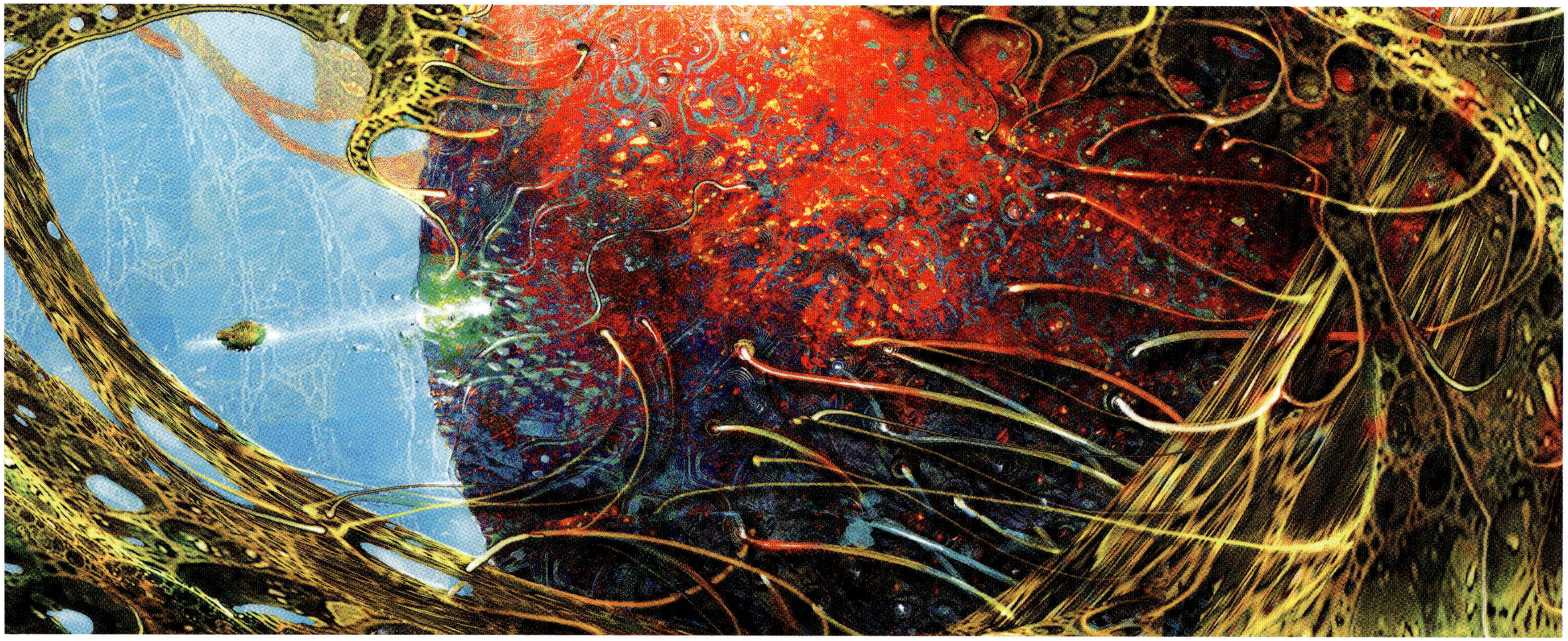

previous DICKENSON

DICKENSON

SZE

SZE

PARK

FUENTEBELLA

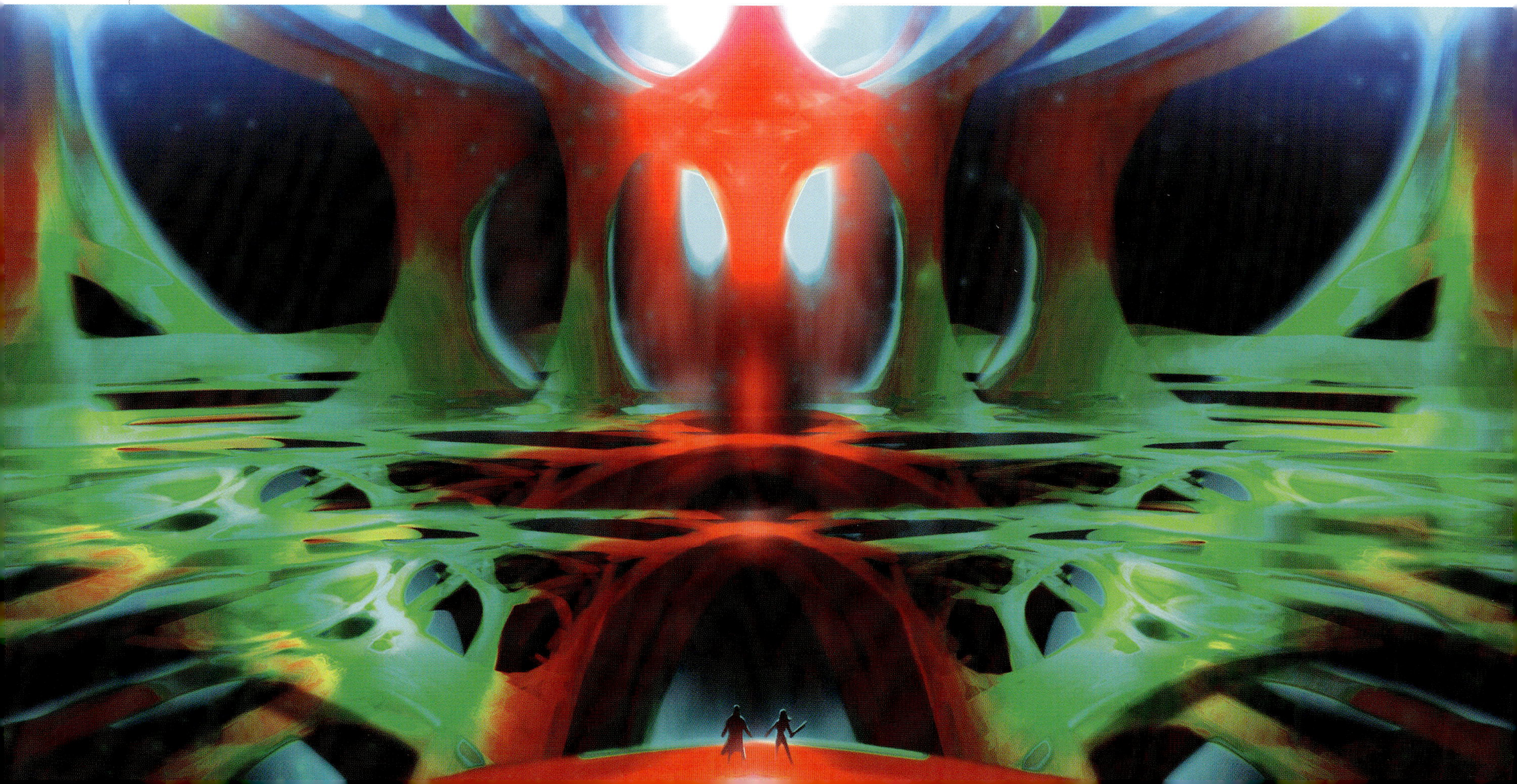

DICKENSON

SZE

REEDER

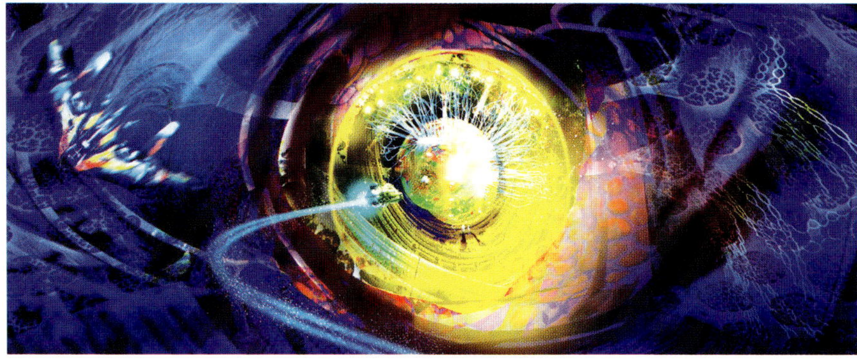

MICHLAP

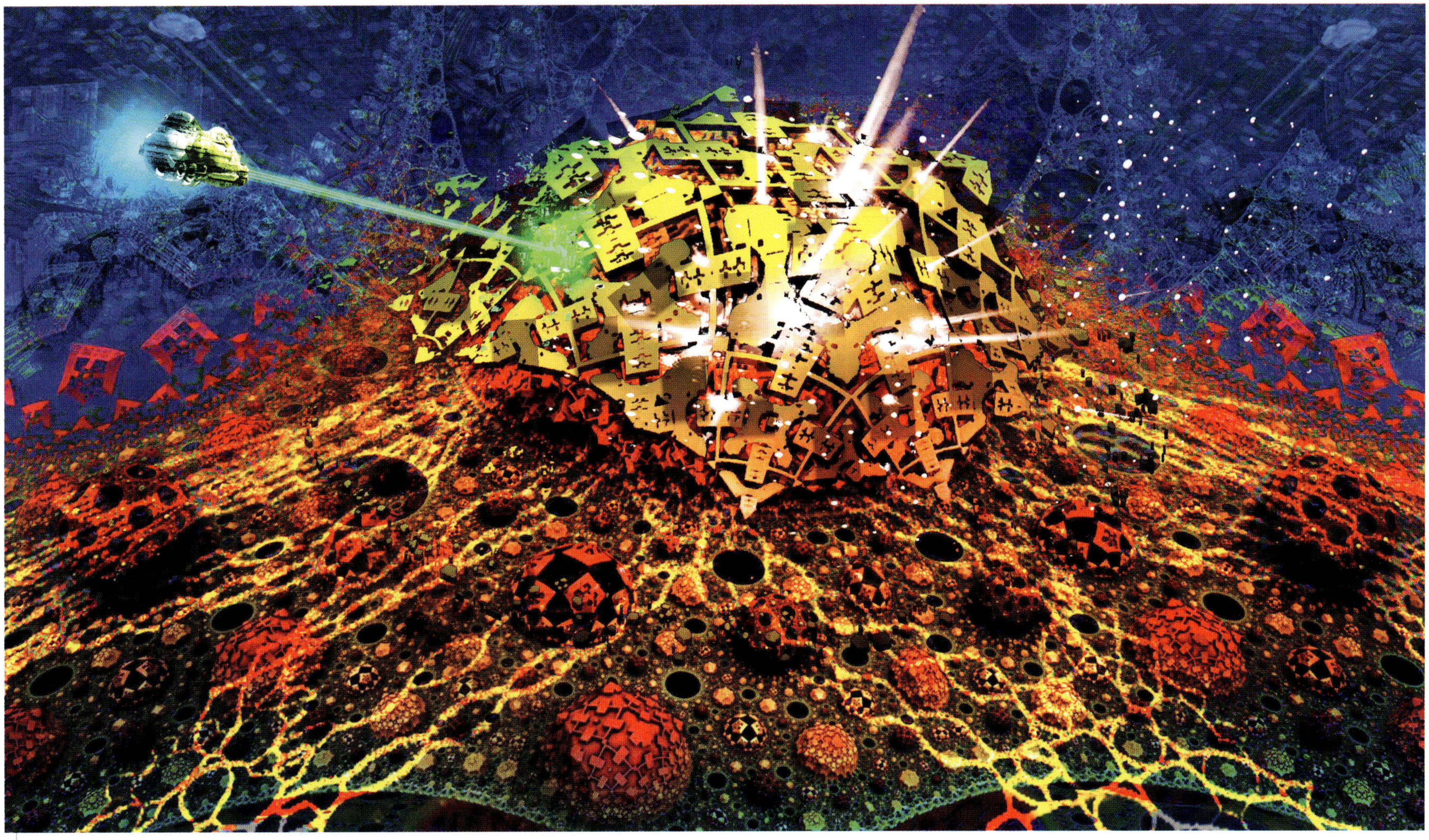

MICHLAP

MICHLAP

DICKENSON

SZE

MICHLAP

EGO'S TRANSFORMATION

"Here I showcased Ego in his environment, being completely at ease and with full control of his being," Visual Development Illustrator Jackson Sze says. "We were trying to figure out if his clothes were grown onto his body like the flora of his planet, so the textures and make here feels organic. Ego is a powerful character, so the symmetric and ornate design of his coat tries to speak to that idea."

previous PARK

SZE

FRANCISCO

PARK

SZE

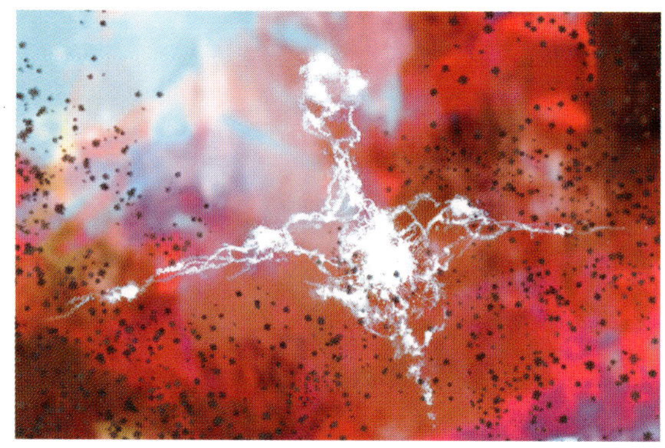

PARK

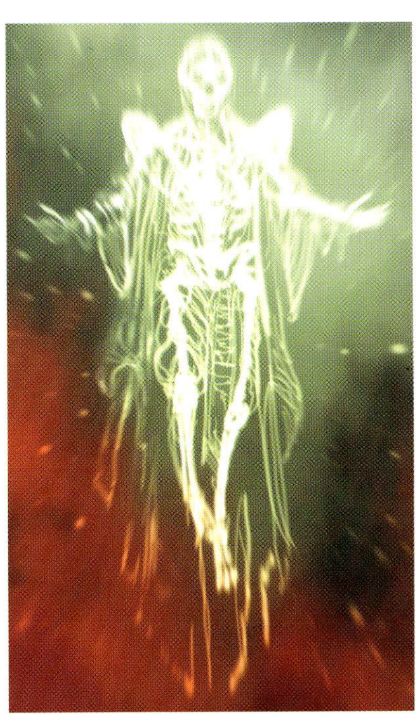

MARANTZ

FUENTEBELLA

"Conceptualizing various power sets, various transformations, for Ego was something I spent a lot of time on," Visual Development Illustrator Rodney Fuentebella says. "As he evolved as a character, as his world evolved, it presented new opportunities for integrating different aesthetics. I wanted him to feel like he was in complete control of everything around him. It made him increasingly dangerous. If everything around him is at his disposal as a weapon, it adds a level of unpredictability to his character."

FUENTEBELLA

SZE

SZE

CHEN

MARANTZ

"It's always fun when you're working with somebody who is the creator, when you're working with someone who understands it better than anyone ever will," actor Kurt Russell says. "I've been fortunate to have many opportunities to do that with writers, directors, and filmmakers who were creating their story. James is that guy. I was always able to ask questions. I was able to create with him, corroborate, collaborate—and do it comfortably, because he's the father. This story is his choice. It came down to some very interesting points of view, ones that I found challenging and was also able to challenge. James has confidence and integrity with glints of openness in his eyes. It made creating a character that much more satisfying, because we were doing it together."

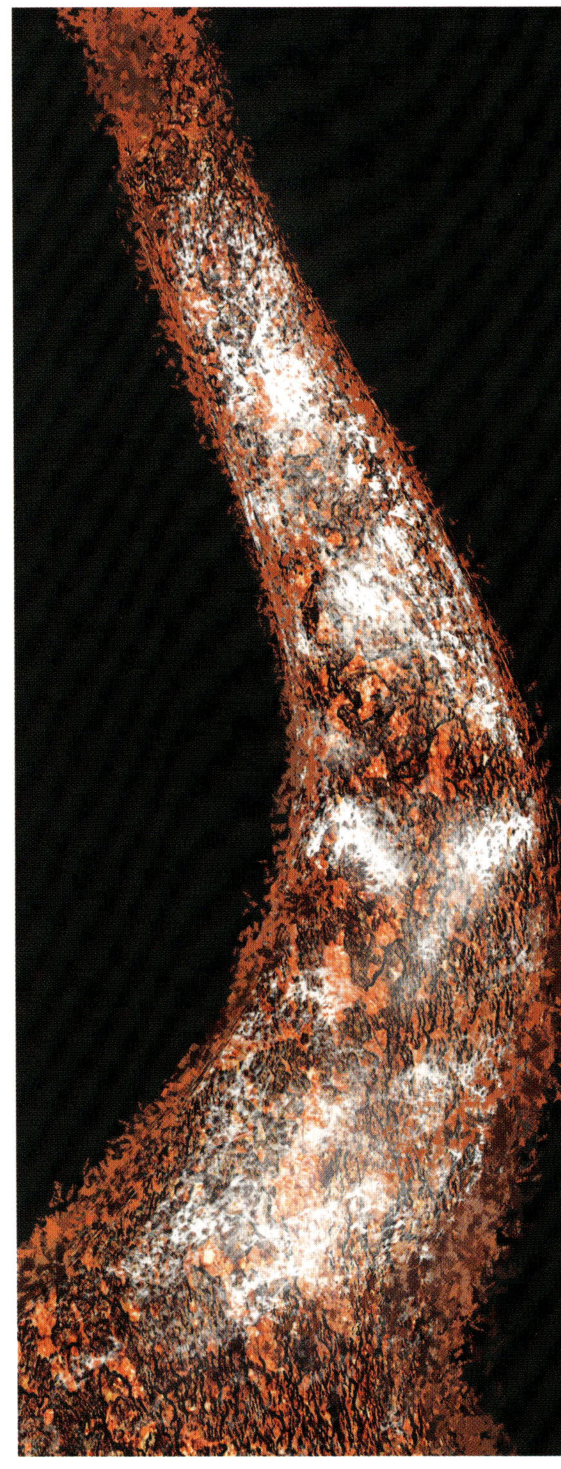

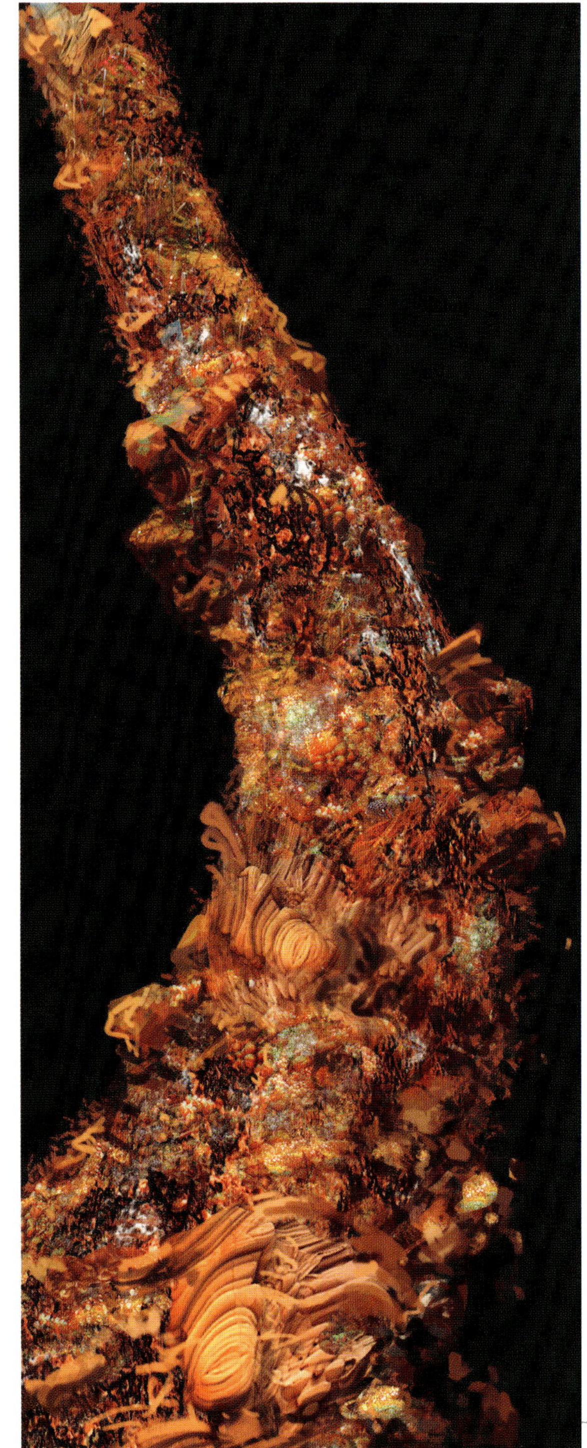

SZE

PETER'S MURAL

"An early draft of the script called for a dramatic moment where a room in Ego's palace begins to shift—more specifically, the wall panels," Jackson Sze says. "As Ego is discussing Quill's past, they begin to display important moments in Quill's life: spending time with his mom, learning from Yondu, genuine family moments with Groot, etc. Since it was an important story moment, I wanted to afford the image a sense of grandeur. The illustration provided an opportunity to showcase what giant sand monuments could look like in an organic Ego environment. My other goal was to make sure the scale was appropriate to the magnitude of what's happening with the story beat."

SZE

REEDER

"James is a profound thinker," Executive Producer Louis D'Esposito says. "He's spiritually grounded, while being generous and balanced with the actors on set. The finale of the film is more than a fight—it's a coming together. It has the pacing and edge-of-your-seat spectacle, but it's accentuated by the growth of the characters within it. The setups that James creates are remarkable and truly speak to his innate ability as a storyteller."

BACH

EAVES

MICHLAP

BACH

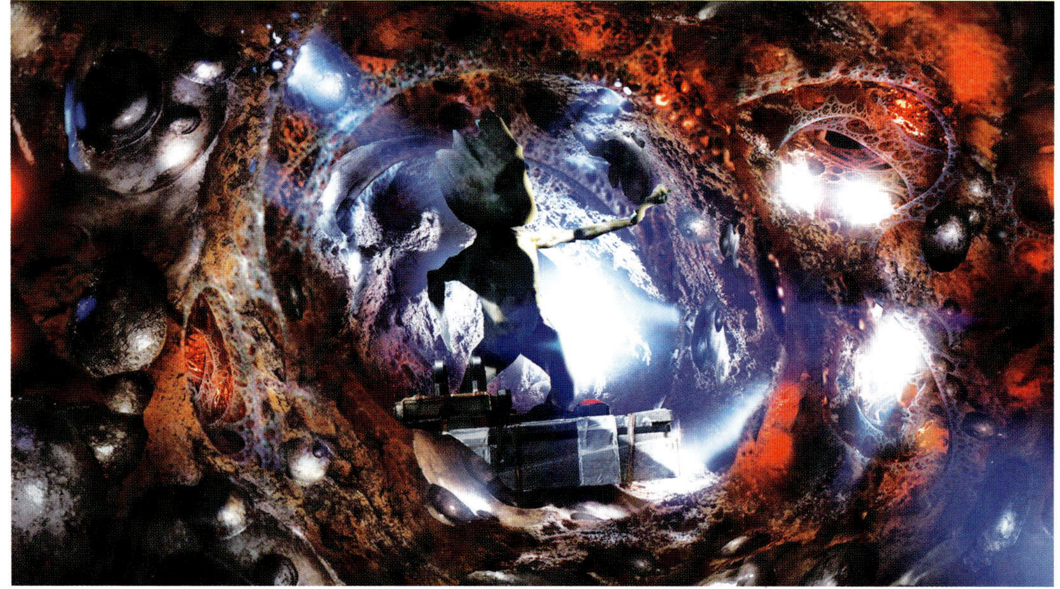

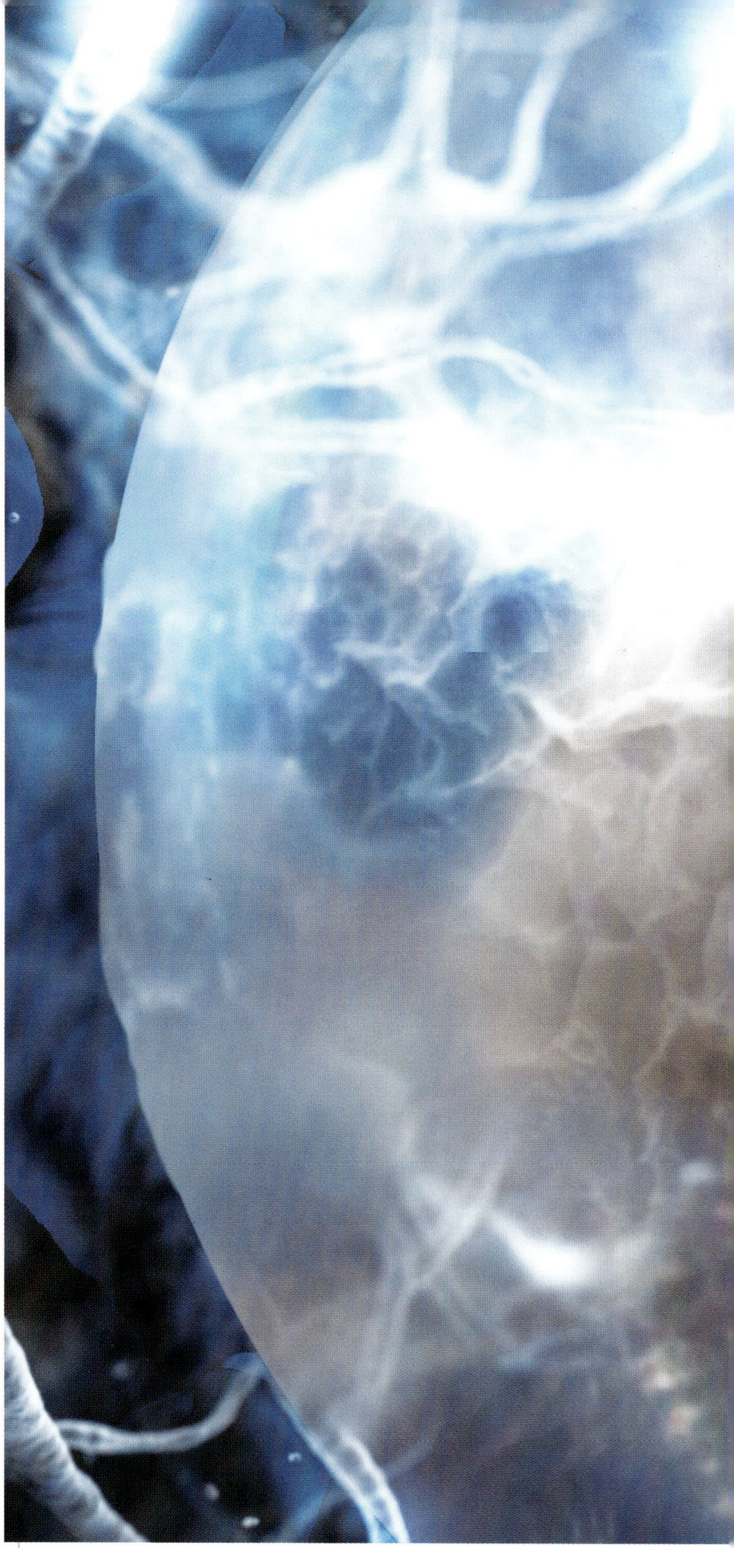

METHOD STUDIOS

"This keyframe was a moment James thought would mirror a similar scenario from the first film, but in reverse," Andy Park says. "In the first film, Groot grabs Rocket and runs away from the explosion. This time, it's Rocket's turn to be the protector."

"My job was mostly to find the right pose, as well as doing the painterly part," Michael Kutsche says. "It's a fine example of true buddy love."

KUTSCHE

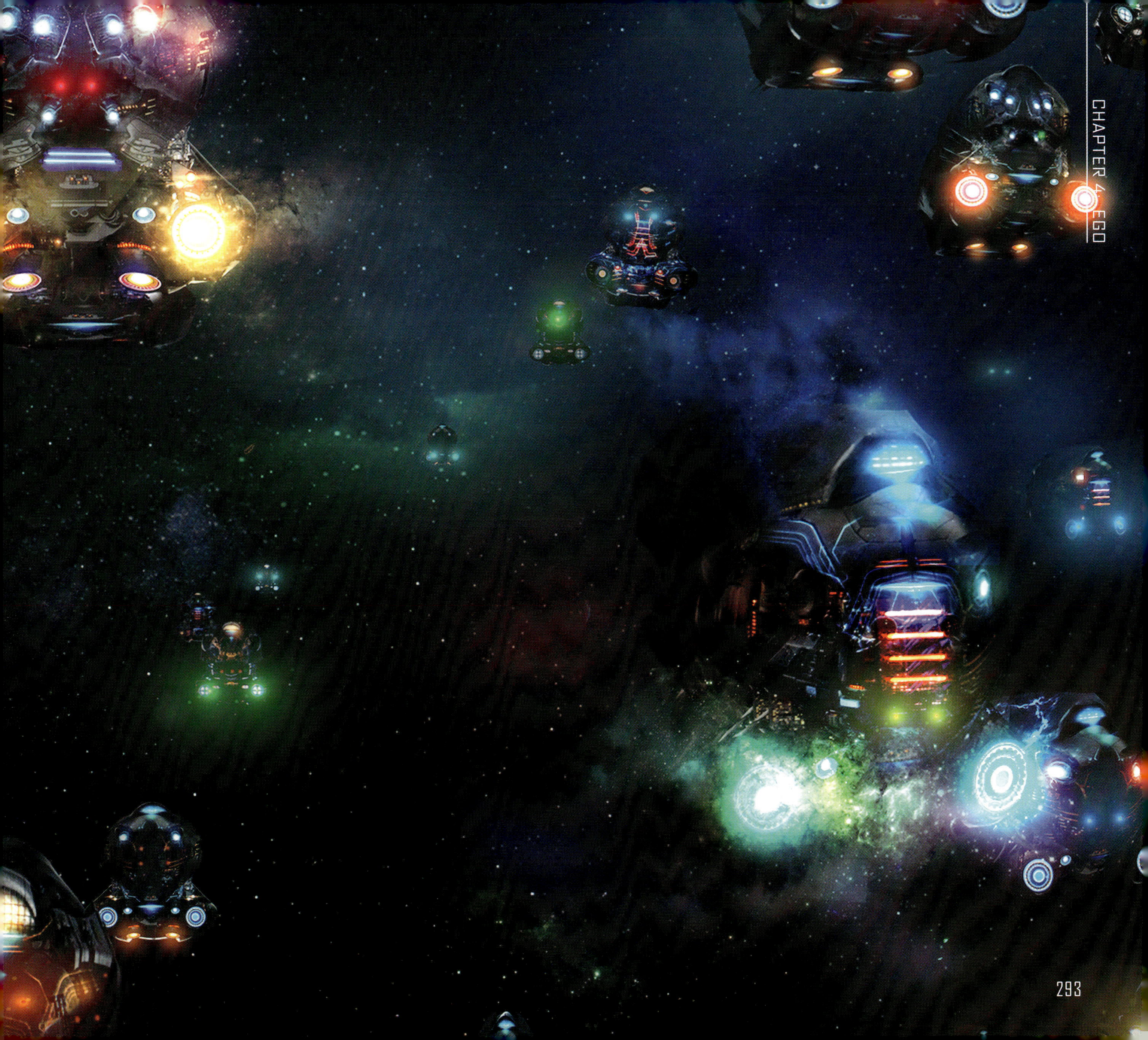

CHAPTER 5
TERRA
MARKETING

SINCE BOLDLY PROCLAIMING "You're Welcome" on the first film's teaser poster, the marketing for *Guardians of the Galaxy* has emphasized attitude, character, and color. "I love creating big movies that people love, but still have heart," Director James Gunn says. "I think that's so rare these days. There are so many big, huge movies that are cookie-cutter and unexciting, with the same archetypes that we've seen time and time again, the same old plots that we've seen time and time again. It really excites me that we can offer something different to people, that we can offer something a little bit more honest."

Since the inception of the Marvel Cinematic Universe, its connective tissue and overlapping storylines have contributed significantly its success. But like the film's marketing, *Guardians of the Galaxy Vol. 2* marches to the beat of its own drum. "The point of this story has nothing to do with the MCU," Gunn says. "I was given nothing by Marvel to have to tie into this time around—which I'm really happy about, because it's about creating a self-enclosed story that could be one movie or could be a billion, and that's what this film is. It's definitely attached to the MCU, but that has nothing to do with the story."

previous METHOD STUDIOS

BLT COMMUNICATIONS

The first piece of concept art for *Guardians of the Galaxy Vol. 2* was revealed at the 2015 San Diego Comic-Con. Illustrated by Visual Development Supervisor Andy Park, the image showcases the film's returning characters, as well as newcomer Mantis. "This keyframe depicts a moment within the planet's belly where they assemble together to fend off the evil that threatens to destroy the galaxy as we know it (of course!)," Park says. "It essentially also welcomes Mantis and Yondu to the team. For all intents and purposes, this image is...*Guardians of the Galaxy 2.0*."

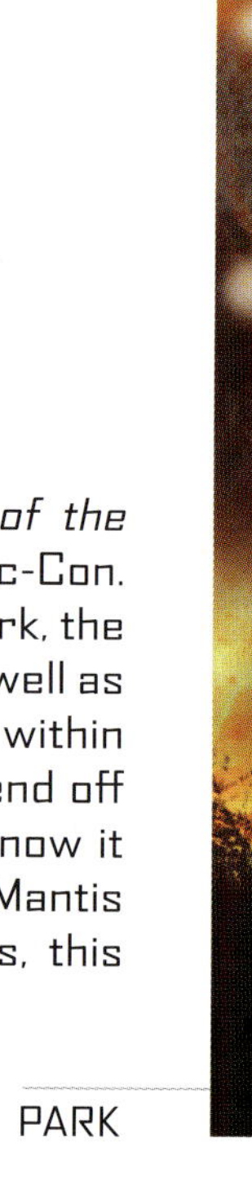

PARK

JULY 2015
WWW.FB.COM/ANTMAN
PRODUCTION CONCEPT ART
MARVEL
©2014 MARVEL

THEATRICAL TEASER POSTERS

SZE

RAVAGERS THANK-YOU NOTE

"This image was done as a thank-you note to the Ravager actors who went to Marvel Studios' Hall H panel at San Diego Comic-Con 2016," Visual Development Illustrator Jackson Sze says. "The Ravagers did a hilarious skit with James Gunn to introduce the *Guardians of the Galaxy Vol. 2* segment of the panel. I thought a postcard would be a fun way to say thank you, and made sure to include the San Diego Convention Center to mark the location of the event."

CONCEPT ART

BLT COMMUNICATIONS

BLT COMMUNICATIONS
and DEANNA ADONA

AFTERWORD 2017

GUARDIANS OF THE GALAXY IS RISKY.

BUT THEN AGAIN, Marvel Studios is in the business of being risky. From its inception, Marvel Studios set out to create what no other studio in history had attempted: a connected universe of films called the Marvel Cinematic Universe. It was a model that every comic-book reader was familiar with. In our youth, we read the stories of our favorite individual heroes, and occasionally they would appear in each other's books and even team up as a group in yet another team book. It's a pretty simple concept, but only possible on paper. Or so we thought. In May of 2012, *Marvel's The Avengers* hit theaters, and the impossible became a reality.

After that massive success, we were told that one of our next movies would be Guardians of the Galaxy. There was a collective reaction of confusion (and laughter) amongst us in the Visual Development Department. I grew up an avid Marvel Comics reader, but even I barely knew who these characters were. "What?" "No way!" "Are you serious?" They were.

It turned out to be one of the most amazing projects in our studio's history. It opened up the Marvel Cinematic Universe well beyond anything we had done up to that point. The Thor films certainly began this exploration into other realms, but *Guardians of the Galaxy* blew the top off when it came to the possibilities. We didn't have to be safe or contained anymore. I will admit that at first it felt like this could be our version of Star Wars, but with the leadership of James Gunn, it became completely its own thing. It was fresh and unique.

Guardians of the Galaxy premiered in May of 2014 and became a game-changing type of movie. And this was immediately after the game changer that was *Marvel's The Avengers*. But this hit was very different. The industry and the fans embraced this eclectic band of misfits, and what was once a completely unknown property had, in an instant, become a household name. Everyone now knew what "I am Groot" meant.

In 2015, I became the visual development supervisor of the sequel to this now-juggernaut franchise. Our department's job was to create the look of the characters in *Guardians of the Galaxy Vol. 2* and to illustrate key moments to help visualize the film's look and feel for the film. James Gunn had a clear vision and bold direction for this sequel. He finds that rare combination of humor, heart, and wackiness that makes this crazy concept work. This type of film needs that balance of not taking itself too seriously and yet absolutely taking itself seriously that James does so well with all his films. As the writer and director, he knows these characters better than anyone. He knows comic books. He knows how to tell a story. And he knows how to make people feel. It was an honor to work closely with him, finding the looks of the characters we already know and love, as well as discovering the looks of the many new characters we would encounter in this film. His concern wasn't so much to replicate the magic of the first film, but to expand and explore the world and characters he's grown to love. That passion was contagious.

I've worked at Marvel Studios for seven years, and it's been an absolute honor to work on so many amazing films. And I completely recognize that the number-one reason for the success of our studio goes first and foremost to the leadership of Kevin Feige. He's that perfect combination of comic-book fan who knows what makes comic books great and great filmmaker who knows how to make a good film. He's making films that he wants to see as a fan. That's how I approach my concept art on these films. I respect the source material, and I want to give the audience what they've been craving to see for so many years. Kevin understands this all too well. Then there's Louis D'Esposito and Victoria Alonzo. They are the other two captains of the ship that is Marvel Studios. It is their leadership that has allowed the studio to have almost a decade's worth of number-one hits that have simply changed the whole industry.

On this film, I had the distinct pleasure of working with some of the best talent in the industry: Production Designer Scott Chambliss, Visual Effects Supervisor Chris Townsend, Costume Designer Judianna Makovsky, Executive Producer Jonathan Schwartz, Assistant to Executive Producer Mary Livanos, Associate Producer Simon Hatt, Visual Development Producer Jacob Johnston, Visual Development Manager AJ Vargas, Visual Development Coordinator Bojan Vucicevic, and the rest of the incredible staff at Marvel Studios. Making films is definitely a collaborative effort, and it was a pleasure to work with each of these amazing talents.

I'd be remiss not to acknowledge the amazing group of artists I got to work with on this film. Like in every film, we painted up hundreds of images trying to design the looks of the various characters. Some characters got approved by James [Gunn] and the top brass at Marvel fairly quickly, while others required a lot of exploration. Ego was an example of a character that took quite a while to get approved. A lot of that was due to the evolving storyline, as well as the importance of the character and his effect on the looks of so many other aspects of the film. Other characters like Mantis surprisingly found a look that was agreed upon fairly early in the process. Our job is to design characters that will not only look great on screen, but that will ultimately serve the story. My team of artists went above and beyond on this project, and I couldn't be more proud of them. I'm a lucky guy because I get to work with some of the best concept artists in the business. A huge thank you goes out to: Jackson Sze, Rodney Fuentebella, Anthony Francisco, Jerad Marantz, Kevin Chen, Justin Sweet, Michael Kutsche, Ian Joyner, Tully Summers, Melissa Encinas, and Constantine Sekeris. I have to give a big shout-out to my former leader on the first *Guardians of the Galaxy*, Charlie Wen. I learned so much from him, and I see him as my mentor and my good friend. And I'd like to thank our Head of Visual Development Ryan Meinerding. He's been with Marvel Studios since day one, and this department wouldn't exist if it weren't for him. His talent inspires me every day.

Guardians of the Galaxy was risky. It's not anymore. But what James [Gunn] has created with this sequel is not playing it safe by any means. He went all out on this one, and it has that magic that will make people love these a-holes (and some new a-holes) even more. So what's next for Marvel Studios and *Guardians of the Galaxy*? Something risky, of course. I can't wait.

Park

ANDY PARK

DIRECTOR JAMES GUNN began his filmmaking career with an eight-millimeter camera at the age of 12. His first film featured his brother Sean—later an actor on the WB's *The Gilmore Girls*—being disemboweled by zombies. While attending Columbia University, Gunn applied for a part-time job filing papers at famed B-movie studio Troma Entertainment and ended up writing the screenplay for the movie *Tromeo & Juliet* instead—for $150. In 1997, *Tromeo* became a cult hit. In 2000, Gunn wrote and starred in *The Specials*, a film about a group of super heroes on their day off. In the same year, Bloomsbury Press released Gunn's critically acclaimed novel *The Toy Collector*. He also wrote, with Lloyd Kaufman, the nonfiction book *All I Need To Know About Filmmaking I Learned From The Toxic Avenger*. Gunn wrote the screenplay for the 2002 film *Scooby-Doo*, and in March of 2004, Gunn became the first screenwriter in cinema history to write back-to-back #1-for-the-weekend box-office hits, with the critically acclaimed, re-imagined *Dawn of the Dead* and *Scooby-Doo: Monsters Unleashed*. Gunn's love for the comedy and horror genres coalesced in 2006's humorous horror film *Slither*. Gunn wrote the film, his feature-film directorial debut, which was named "The Best Horror film of 2006" by *Rue Morgue* magazine, and Gunn won a Saturn Award and a Fangoria Chainsaw Award for his work on the film. In 2008, Gunn created Xbox Live's first original content, including his own *Sparky & Mikaela*. Also in 2008, Gunn hosted the reality show *Scream Queens* for VH1. Gunn most recently wrote and directed the independent feature film *Super*, which was an official selection at the Toronto Film Festival, was picked up by IFC Films, and is IFC's top-selling film on On Demand. In 2012, Gunn released his first video game, *Lollipop Chainsaw*, with Suda 51 and Warner Bros., on Xbox and PlayStation 3.

Over the past decade, PRODUCER AND MARVEL STUDIOS PRESIDENT KEVIN FEIGE has played an instrumental role in a string of blockbuster feature films adapted from the pages of Marvel comic books. In his current role, Feige oversees all creative aspects of the company's feature film and home entertainment activities. He is currently producing *Guardians of the Galaxy Vol. 2* and *Thor: Ragnarok*, which will hit theaters in 2017; *Black Panther*, *Avengers: Infinity War*, and *Ant-Man and the Wasp*, which will be released in 2018; and *Captain Marvel* and the fourth *Avengers* film, which will be in theaters in 2019. In 2016, Feige produced *Captain America: Civil War*, which crossed $1 billion in global box office and was the year's highest-grossing film, and *Doctor Strange*, which grossed more than $600 million worldwide. His previous producing credits for Marvel include *Iron Man 3*, *Marvel's The Avengers*, *Ant-Man*, *Avengers: Age of Ultron*, *Guardians of the Galaxy*, *Captain America: The Winter Soldier*, *Thor: The Dark World*, *Thor*, *Captain America: The First Avenger*, *Iron Man 2*, and *Iron Man*.

EXECUTIVE PRODUCER AND MARVEL STUDIOS CO-PRESIDENT LOUIS D'ESPOSITO served as executive producer on the blockbuster hits *Iron Man*, *Iron Man 2*, *Thor*, *Captain America: The First Avenger*, *Marvel's The Avengers*, *Iron Man 3*, *Thor: The Dark World*, *Captain America: The Winter Soldier*, *Guardians of the Galaxy*, and most recently *Captain America: Civil War*, *Avengers: Age of Ultron*, *Ant-Man*, and *Doctor Strange*. He is currently working on the highly anticipated films *Thor: Ragnarok*, *Guardians of the Galaxy Vol. 2*, *Black Panther*, *Ant-Man and the Wasp*, *Captain Marvel and Avengers: Infinity War*, as well as collaborating with Marvel Studios' President Kevin Feige to build the future Marvel slate. As co-president of the studio and executive producer on all Marvel films, D'Esposito balances running the studio with overseeing each film from its development stage to distribution. In addition to executive-producing Marvel Studios' films, D'Esposito directed the Marvel One-Shot *Item 47*, which made its debut to fans at the 2012 San Diego Comic-Con International and was featured again at the LA Shorts Fest in September 2012. The project was released as an added feature on *Marvel's The Avengers* Blu-ray disc. D'Esposito also directed the second Marvel One-Shot *Agent Carter*, starring Hayley Atwell, which premiered at the 2013 San Diego Comic-Con to critical praise from press and fans, and is an added feature on the *Iron Man 3* Blu-ray disc. The One-Shot's popularity led to development of the TV series *Marvel's Agent Carter*. D'Esposito began his tenure at Marvel Studios in 2006. Prior to Marvel, D'Esposito's executive-producing credits include the 2006 hit film *The Pursuit of Happyness*, starring Will Smith; *Zathura: A Space Adventure*; and the 2003 hit *S.W.A.T.*, starring Samuel L. Jackson and Colin Farrell.

Marvel Studios EXECUTIVE VICE PRESIDENT OF PHYSICAL PRODUCTION VICTORIA ALONSO is executive-producing James Gunn's *Guardians of the Galaxy Vol. 2*, Jon Watt's *Spider-Man: Homecoming*, and Taika Waititi's *Thor: Ragnarok*. In her executive role, she oversees postproduction and visual effects for the studio slate. She executive-produced Scott Derrickson's *Doctor Strange*, Joe and Anthony Russo's *Captain America: Civil War*, Peyton Reed's *Ant-Man*, Joss Whedon's *Avengers: Age of Ultron*, James Gunn's *Guardians of the Galaxy*, Joe and Anthony Russo's *Captain America: The Winter Soldier*, Alan Taylor's *Thor: The Dark World*, Shane Black's *Iron Man 3*, and Joss Whedon's *Marvel's The Avengers*. She co-produced Jon Favreau's *Iron Man* and *Iron Man 2*, Kenneth Branagh's *Thor*, and Joe Johnston's *Captain America: The First Avenger*. Alonso's career began at the nascency of the visual-effects industry, when she served as a commercial VFX producer. From there, she VFX-produced numerous feature films, working with such directors as Ridley Scott (*Kingdom of Heaven*), Tim Burton (*Big Fish*), and Andrew Adamson (*Shrek*), to name a few. Through the years, her dedication to the industry has been admired and her achievements recognized. In 2015, Alonso was an honoree of the New York Women in Film & Television's Muse Award for Outstanding Vision and Achievement. In January 2017, she received the Advanced Imaging Society's Harold Lloyd Award.

EXECUTIVE PRODUCER AND VICE PRESIDENT OF PRODUCTION AND DEVELOPMENT JONATHAN SCHWARTZ began his career at Marvel Studios in 2008. Schwartz served as Kevin Feige's assistant on *Iron Man 2*, *Thor*, and *Captain America: The First Avenger*, and as creative executive on *Marvel's The Avengers*. *Guardians of the Galaxy* was the first feature film he oversaw for the studio. An alumnus of Pomona College, Schwartz previously worked at the William Morris Agency.

EXECUTIVE PRODUCER NIKOLAS KORDA lists co-producer on Ridley Scott's *Robin Hood* and Chris Weitz's *The Golden Compass* among his credits. As a unit production manager, Korda's credits include Ridley Scott's *Prometheus* (as well as *Robin Hood*), Jonathan Liebesman's *Wrath of the Titans*, Tim Burton's *Charlie and the Chocolate Factory*, Peter Jackson's *Lord of the Rings* trilogy and Stephen Hopkins' *Lost in Space*. He has also worked as an assistant director on films including Tim Burton's *Batman*, Richard Attenborough's *Cry Freedom*, and Jim Henson's *Labyrinth*, as well as *Rambo III* and *Hamburger Hill*. He served as executive producer on *Tarzan* for Warner Bros.

CO-PRODUCER AND VICE PRESIDENT OF PHYSICAL PRODUCTION DAVID J. GRANT joined Marvel Studios in 2008. As associate producer, he oversaw production on *Iron Man 2*, *Thor*, *Marvel's The Avengers*, and *Thor: The Dark World*; as co-producer, he oversaw *Guardians of the Galaxy Vol. 2*, as well as *Guardians of the Galaxy*, *Ant-Man*, and *Doctor Strange*. Current projects include *Thor: Ragnarok*, *Black Panther*, and *Captain Marvel*. Prior to joining Marvel Studios, Grant was a freelance production supervisor, having worked on *Fast and Furious*, *Iron Man*, *Spider-Man 3*, *Guess Who*, and *Spider-Man 2*.

PRODUCTION DESIGNER SCOTT CHAMBLISS has been nominated for several awards for his motion-picture and TV work, and is an Emmy Award winner for his production design of the J.J. Abrams series *Alias*. His feature-film credits include *Tomorrowland*, *Star Trek Into Darkness*, *Star Trek*, *Salt*, *Cowboys & Aliens*, and *Mission: Impossible III*.

COSTUME DESIGNER JUDIANNA MAKOVSKY is a three-time Academy Award nominee whose designs for *Seabiscuit*, *Harry Potter and the Sorcerer's Stone*, and *Pleasantville* have been recognized with Oscar nominations, as well as being honored by her peers with Costume Designers Guild Awards for the latter two films. She also received a BAFTA nomination for *Harry Potter and the Sorcerer's Stone*. Most recently, Makovsky designed the costumes for *The Hunger Games* and *The Last Airbender*, and *Look of Love*. Some of her other credits include *Cirque du Freak*, *X-Men: The Last Stand*, both *National Treasure* films, *The Legend of Bagger Vance*, *Practical Magic*, *Lolita*, *Mr. Brooks*, *A Little Princess*, *The Quick and the Dead*, *The Devil's Advocate*, *White Squall*, *Reversal of Fortune*, and *Great Expectations*. Makovsky has a BFA from the School of the Art Institute of Chicago, and also attended the Goodman School of Drama as well as the MFA program at Yale University School of Drama.

CINEMATOGRAPHER HENRY BRAHAM is known for his expressive style in both large-scale landscape and interiors—and now outer spacep—combined with his innovative approach to filmmaking. Recent credits include *The Legend of Tarzan*—directed by David Yates, and starring Margot Robbie, Alexander Skarsgård, Christoph Waltz, and Samuel L. Jackson—for Warner Bros. Braham's cinematographic career began in 1989 with the British band The KLF, including their road movie *The White Room*. He became a frequent collaborator with director Kirk Jones, as cinematographer on his films *Waking Ned Devine*, *Nanny McPhee*, and *Everybody's Fine*. Braham's other credits include Chris Weitz's *The Golden Compass*, Tony Bill's *Flyboys*, and Stephen Fry's *Bright Young Things*. He has shot a number of short films as well, including cinematography for Neil Gaiman. Braham won a Primetime Emmy Award for Outstanding Cinematography and earned a BAFTA nomination for Best Cinematography for the epic *Shackleton*, starring Kenneth Branagh and directed by Charles Sturridge. Braham's award-winning career in fashion, commercials, and music videos includes cinematography for Mario Testino for Dolce & Gabbana, Burberry, Michael Kors, Issey Miyake, and Lancome, as well as for Nick Knight. Beyond the screen, Braham designed the lighting for the sellout exhibition *Hats: An Anthology by Stephen Jones* for the Victoria and Albert Museum and shot the groundbreaking live transmission of *The Entertainer* to cinemas around the world from the Garrick Theatre, London, for the Kenneth Branagh Theatre Company. Braham is a member of the British Society of Cinematographers and is the cofounder of the Good Hemp Food brand with Glynis Murray.

PROPERTY MASTER RUSSELL BOBBITT's résumé includes all three of Marvel's *Iron Man* films, *Thor*, and *Captain America: The Winter Soldier*, as well as *Oz: The Great and Powerful*, *The Hangover*, *The Hangover Part II*, and J.J. Abrams' *Star Trek*. Tasked with the design, manufacturing, and acquisition of film props, as well as the establishment of prop continuity from scene to scene, Bobbitt has been developing the physical reality of iconic movies for 30 years. He has twice won Hamilton's prestigious "Behind the Camera" Award for Best Property Master. He has also won two Telly Awards for directing. He resides in Los Angeles with his wife, Tracy, and daughter, Jordan.

VISUAL EFFECTS SUPERVISOR CHRISTOPHER TOWNSEND was the overall VFX supervisor on *Guardians of the Galaxy Vol. 2* with Writer/Director James Gunn. Townsend grew up in England, then traveled and worked throughout Asia and Australia before moving to the United States in 1994 to work at Industrial Light & Magic. He worked as an artist and supervisor on influential movies including *Star Wars* (both the rerelease of the original, *A New Hope*, and the prequel trilogy), *Mission: Impossible*, *The Lost World: Jurassic Park*, *A.I.: Artificial Intelligence*, *Hulk*, *Day After Tomorrow*, *The Island*, and the Academy Award-winning *Pirates of the Caribbean: Dead Man's Chest*. In 2007, he became a freelancer and was the VFX supervisor on Walden/New Line's *Journey to the Center of the Earth*, which made the Academy's VFX shortlist; it was the first stereoscopic motion picture shot and released in HD. He supervised on location for Fox's *X-Men Origins: Wolverine*, oversaw the VFX in Europe for Warner Bros.' *Ninja Assassin*, supervised on Fox's *Percy Jackson and the Lightning Thief*, and again made it to the Bake-Offs in 2012 as the VFX supervisor for Marvel's *Captain America: The First Avenger*, with a highlight being the groundbreaking Skinny Steve transformation effects for the title character. He was nominated for an Academy Award for his work on *Iron Man 3*, and again made the Academy's shortlist for his work on *Avengers: Age of Ultron*.

VISUAL DEVELOPMENT SUPERVISOR ANDY PARK studied as an art/illustration major at both UCLA and Art Center College of Design. His career began as a comic-book artist fulfilling a childhood dream and illustrating such titles as *Tomb Raider*, *Excalibur*, and *Uncanny X-Men* for Marvel, DC, and Image Comics, among others. After a decade in the comic-book industry, he made a career switch and began working as a concept artist in video games. He was one of the leading artists designing the various worlds and fantastical characters/creatures of the award-winning *God of War* video game franchise for Sony Computer Entertainment of America. Park joined the Visual Development Department at Marvel Studios in 2010 as a visual development concept artist, designing characters and keyframe illustrations for *Marvel's The Avengers*, *Iron Man 3*, *Captain America: The Winter Soldier*, *Thor: The Dark World*, *Guardians of the Galaxy*, *Avengers: Age of Ultron*, *Ant-Man*, and *Captain America: Civil War*. He is also serving as the visual development supervisor on the upcoming films *Thor: Ragnarok* and *Ant-Man and the Wasp*.

VISUAL DEVELOPMENT ILLUSTRATOR JACKSON SZE has worked in advertising, video games, television, and film for studios such as Lucasfilm Animation and Sony Computer Entertainment of America. He is a founding member of the BATTLE MiLK series of art books and is a senior concept illustrator at Marvel Studios. He has also taught at Concept Design Academy and Gnomon School of Visual Effects in Hollywood. His credits include *Star Wars: The Clone Wars*, *The Little Prince*, *Marvel's The Avengers*, *Guardians of the Galaxy*, *Guardians of the Galaxy Vol. 2*, *Ant-Man*, *Doctor Strange*, and the upcoming *Thor: Ragnarok*.

VISUAL DEVELOPMENT ILLUSTRATOR RODNEY FUENTEBELLA has degrees in design from UCLA and product design from the Art Center College of Design. Born in the Philippines and raised in San Francisco, he has worked on various projects for Electronic Arts, Atari, Rhythm and Hues, DreamWorks Animation, and *WIRED* magazine, as well as various other entertainment and commercial projects. In film, he worked as a concept artist at Rhythm and Hues before joining the Visual Development team at Marvel Studios. Fuentebella has created key-art illustrations and character designs for various projects including *Captain America: The First Avenger*, *Marvel's The Avengers*, *Iron Man 3*, *Captain America: The Winter Soldier*, *Guardians of the Galaxy*, *Avengers: Age of Ultron*, *Ant-Man*, *Captain America: Civil War*, *Doctor Strange*, *Spider-Man: Homecoming*, *Black Panther*, and other upcoming MCU films.

VISUAL DEVELOPMENT ILLUSTRATOR ANTHONY FRANCISCO started his career working for various effects houses such as Stan Winston Studios, Rick Baker, ADI, Harlow FX, and Illusion Industries. Francisco produced art for *Superman Returns*, *A.I. Artificial Intelligence*, *Men in Black 2*, *Spider-Man*, *The Passion of the Christ*, and *The Chronicles of Riddick*, among others. From 2004-2006, he worked as a concept artist at NCsoft Santa Monica on the *Guild Wars* and *Tabula Rasa* MMO game titles. In 2006, Francisco joined the team at Offset Software as lead concept artist to work on a fantasy-based FPS game. In 2010, he left the game industry to work at Rhythm & Hues Studios on *The Hunger Games*, *R.I.P.D.*, and *Seventh Son*. Francisco also has taught at Gnomon School for Visual Effects, Art Center College of Design in Pasadena, Concept Design Academy, and CGMW online. In late 2012, he joined the Visual Development team at Marvel Studios. His first project was *Guardians of the Galaxy*, in which he had the opportunity to concept-design Baby Groot. Other projects include *Ant-Man*, *Doctor Strange*, *Thor: Ragnarok*, *Avengers: Infinity War*, and *Black Panther*.

STORYBOARD ARTIST DARRIN DENLINGER taught himself to draw by copying Marvel Comics covers all through middle school. After he watched *Superman: The Movie* and *Alien* as a teenager, the twin passions of art and cinema sent him on a twisty journey studying film production at San Diego State University, and spending years learning the inner workings of Hollywood in a variety of positions at Universal Studios and Sony Pictures. When his friend George Huang offered him a chance to do storyboards on his teen comedy *Trojan War*, Denlinger had found his calling. He has contributed to a variety of films, from *Pirates of the Caribbean* to *Bridesmaids*. Considering his childhood fixation with comic-book covers, his tenure on Marvel films such as *The Incredible Hulk*, *Thor*, *Captain America: The First Avenger*, *Marvel's The Avengers*, *Iron Man 3*, *Avengers: Age of Ultron*, *Captain America: Civil War*, *Doctor Strange*, and the upcoming *Avengers: Infinity War* has been a dream come true.

A C K N O W L

Deanna Adona
Victoria Alonso
Bryan Andrews
Jonathan Bach
Laurent Ben-Mimoun
BLT Communications
Russell Bobbitt

Phillip Boutte Jr.
Henry Braham
John Byrne
Scott Chambliss
Kevin Chen
Christian Cordella
Wes Craig

Louis D'Esposito
John Dell
Matt Delmanowski
Darrin Denlinger
Erika Denton
Mariano A. Diaz
John Dickenson

Andrea Dopaso
John Eaves
Nathan Fairbairn
Kevin Feige
Anthony Francisco
Rodney Fuentebella
David J. Grant

James Gunn
Sean Hargreaves
Simon Hatt
Andrew Hennessy
Josh Herman
Joe Hiura
George Hull

Elissa Hunter
Ian Joyner
Tex Kadonaga
Alexei Krassovsky
David Krentz
Michael Kutsche
Fritz Lang

D G M E N T S

TRIXTER

Percival Lanuza
Serge LaPointe
Legacy Effects
Mary Livanos
Scott Lukowski
Judianna Makovsky
Jerad Marantz

Victor Martinez
Iain McFadyen
Steve McNiven
Ryan Meinerding
Method Studios
Samuel Michlap
Luca Nemolato

Till Nowak
Andy Park
Avia Perez
Justin Ponsor
Jacque Porte
Ryan Potter
Will Quintana

Andrew Reeder
Alex Ross
Jonathan Schwartz
Constantine Sekeris
Craig Sellars
Bob Sharen
Dean Sherriff

Gloria Shih
Tully Summers
Justin Sweet
Jackson Sze
Pete Thompson
Christopher Townsend
Trixter

A.J. Vargas
Bojan Vucicevic
Brad Walker
Tyler West

ARTIST CREDITS

Deanna Adona
Page 303

Jonathan Bach
Gatefold
Pages 130-131, 133, 174-175, 198-199, 202-203, 206-207, 289

Laurent Ben-Mimoun
Page 132

BLT Communications
Pages 296-297, 302-303

Phillip Boutte Jr.
Page 61

John Byrne
Page 10

Kevin Chen
Pages 50-55, 57, 58-59, 99, 276, 280-281

Christian Cordella
Pages 18-19, 24-25, 26, 62, 65, 98

Wes Craig
Page 12

John Dell
Page 11

Darrin Denlinger
Gatefold

Mariano A. Diaz
Pages 29, 36, 71, 125, 140-141, 143

John Dickenson
Pages 2-3, 204, 204-205, 226-229, 232-239, 246, 251-255, 258, 262

Andrea Dopaso
Pages 84-85, 87, 89, 219

John Eaves
Pages 16, 22-23, 26, 28-29, 87, 124-125, 289

Nathan Fairbairn
Page 12

Anthony Francisco
Pages 30-33, 34-36, 44, 95, 97, 98, 102-105, 142-145, 158, 162, 211, 266-267, 310-311

Rodney Fuentebella
Pages 4-5, 18-19, 72-73, 76-79, 100-101, 118, 138-139, 150-153, 155, 220-225, 257, 274

Sean Hargreaves
Pages 90, 139

Andrew Hennessy
Page 12

Josh Herman
Pages 35, 72, 98

Joe Hiura
Pages 240, 242-243

George Hull
Pages 180-181, 182-183, 240-243

Ian Joyner
Pages 154, 164, 166, 307

Tex Kadonaga
Pages 174-175

Michael Kutsche
Gatefold

Pages 27, 72, 134, 292-293

Fritz Lang
Pages 148-149

Serge LaPointe
Page 12

Legacy Effects
Pages 116-117, 142

Scott Lukowski
Pages 130-131

Jerad Marantz
Pages 46-47, 119, 147, 273, 278-279

Victor Martinez
Pages 175, 208-209

Iain McFadyen
Pages 40-41

Steve McNiven
Page 11

Ryan Meinerding
Pages 148-149

Method Studios
Pages 37, 80-81, 86, 90-91, 135, 194-197, 290-291, 294-295

Samuel Michlap
Pages 192-194, 198-201, 203, 210-215, 238-239, 244-245, 246-250, 260-263, 288

Luca Nemolato
Page 117

Till Nowak
Pages 40-43, 45, 66-69, 74-77, 216, 218, 307

Andy Park
Cover
Pages 16-17, 20-24, 45, 48-49, 63-64, 99, 106-115, 176, 256, 268-269, 272, 298-299, 304-305

Justin Ponsor
Page 11

Will Quintana
Page 12

Andrew Reeder
Pages 88-89, 260, 288

Alex Ross
Page 13

Alex Scharf
Gatefold

Constantine Sekeris
Page 165

Craig Sellars
Pages 14-15, 38-39, 40-41, 50-51, 60, 132, 188-189, 190, 216-219, 241

Bob Sharen
Page 10

Dean Sherriff
Pages 133, 170-171, 172-173, 177, 184-185, 190, 241

Gloria Shih
Pages 55, 56, 60, 70

Tully Summers
Pages 157, 160-161, 163, 166-167

Justin Sweet
Pages 56, 146, 282-283

Jackson Sze
Pages 17, 28-29, 82-83, 92-94, 96, 99, 101, 103-104, 119-123, 126-127, 133, 137, 158-159, 162, 166, 178-179, 186-187, 230-231, 256, 258-259, 264-265, 270-271, 274-275, 276, 284-287, 301

Pete Thompson
Pages 168-169, 170

Trixter
Pages 87, 116, 125, 132-133, 136, 156-157, 166, 191, 308-309

Brad Walker
Page 12

Tyler West
Page 183

FRANCISCO

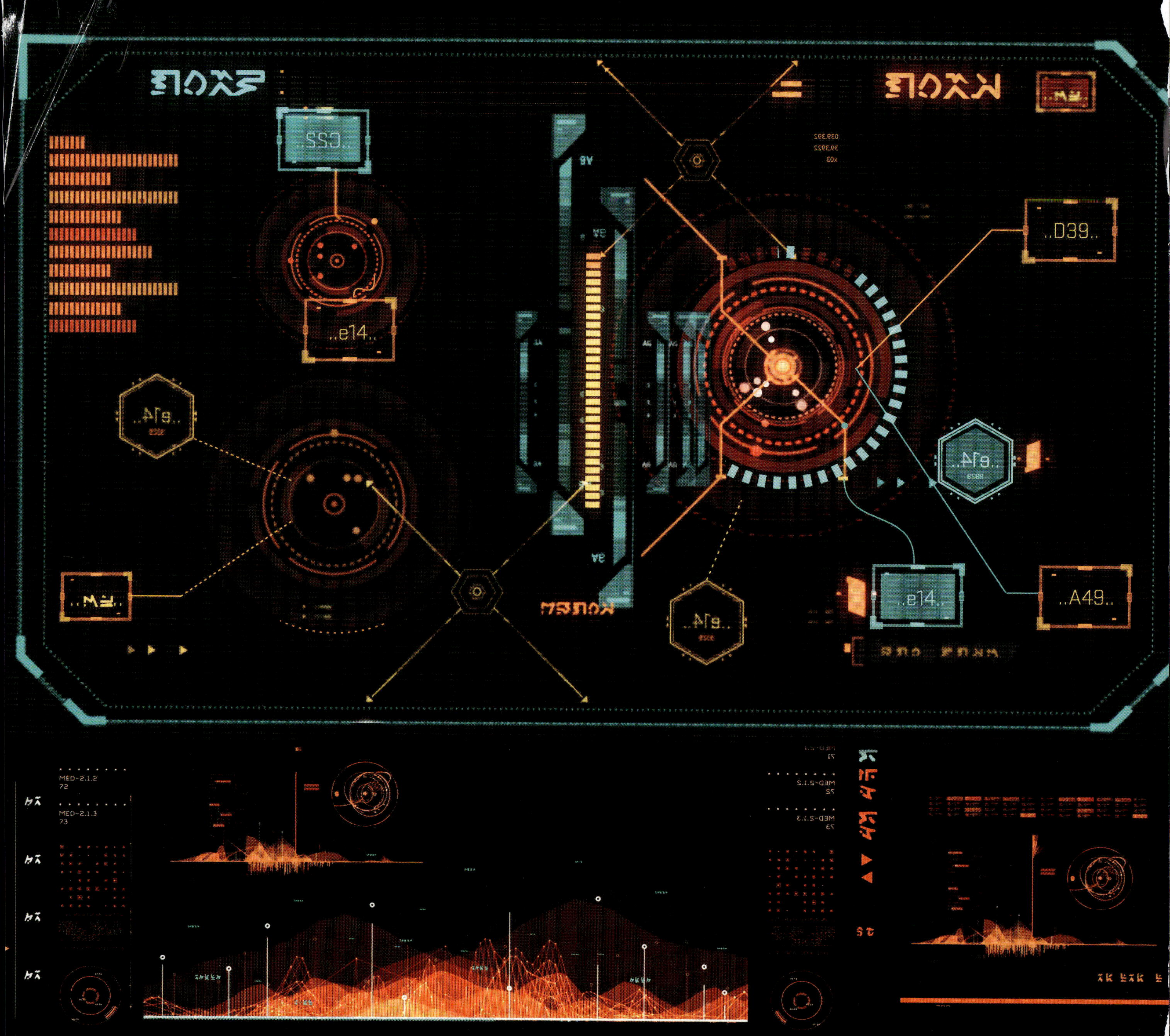
..D39..
..e14..
..A49..
MED-2.1.2
72
MED-2.1.3
73